CARROLL COLLEGE LIBRARY
WAUKESHA, WISCONSIN 53186

D0843118

How Much Do
National Borders
Matter?

Integrating National Economies: Promise and Pitfalls

Robert Z. Lawrence (Harvard University), Albert Bressand (Promethee), and
Takatoshi Ito (Hitotsubashi University)
A VISION FOR THE WORLD ECONOMY: OPENNESS, DIVERSITY, AND COHESION

Barry Bosworth (Brookings Institution) and Gur Ofer (Hebrew University)
Reforming Planned Economies in an Integrating World Economy

Ralph C. Bryant (Brookings Institution)
International Coordination of National Stabilization Policies

Richard N. Cooper (Harvard University)
Environment and Resource Policies for the World Economy

Ronald G. Ehrenberg (Cornell University)
Labor Markets and Integrating National Economies

Barry Eichengreen (University of California, Berkeley)
International Monetary Arrangements for the 21st Century

Mitsuhiro Fukao (Bank of Japan)
**Financial Integration, Corporate Governance, and the Performance of
Multinational Companies**

Stephan Haggard (University of California, San Diego)
Developing Nations and the Politics of Global Integration

John F. Helliwell
How Much Do National Borders Matter?

Richard J. Herring (University of Pennsylvania) and Robert E. Litan
(Department of Justice/Brookings Institution)
Financial Regulation in the Global Economy

Miles Kahler (University of California, San Diego)
International Institutions and the Political Economy of Integration

Anne O. Krueger (Stanford University)
Trade Policies and Developing Nations

Robert Z. Lawrence (Harvard University)
Regionalism, Multilateralism, and Deeper Integration

Sylvia Ostry (University of Toronto) and Richard R. Nelson (Columbia University)
Techno-Nationalism and Techno-Globalism: Conflict and Cooperation

Robert L. Paarlberg (Wellesley College/Harvard University)
**Leadership Abroad Begins at Home: U.S. Foreign Economic Policy after
the Cold War**

F. M. Scherer (Harvard University)
Competition Policies for an Integrated World Economy

Susan L. Shirk (University of California, San Diego)
**How China Opened Its Door: The Political Success of the PRC's Foreign
Trade and Investment Reforms**

Alan O. Sykes (University of Chicago)
Product Standards for Internationally Integrated Goods Markets

Akihiko Tanaka (Institute of Oriental Culture, University of Tokyo)
The Politics of Deeper Integration: National Attitudes and Policies in Japan

Vito Tanzi (International Monetary Fund)
Taxation in an Integrating World

William Wallace (St. Antony's College, Oxford University)
Regional Integration: The West European Experience

John F. Helliwell

How Much Do National Borders Matter?

HF
3226
.5
.H45
1998

BROOKINGS INSTITUTION PRESS
Washington, D.C.

Copyright © 1998
THE BROOKINGS INSTITUTION
1775 Massachusetts Avenue, N.W., Washington, D.C. 20036

All rights reserved

Library of Congress Cataloging-in-Publication data:
Helliwell, John F.
How much do national borders matter? /
John F. Helliwell.
p. cm.
Includes bibiliographical references.
ISBN 0-8157-3554-5 (cloth: permanent paper)
ISBN 0-8157-3553-7 (pbk.: permanent paper)
1. Canada—Commerce. 2. United States—Commerce.
3. Canada—Commerce—United States. 4. United
States—Commerce—Canada. 5. Interstate commerce—Canada.
6. Interstate commerce—United States. 7. Boundaries.
8. International trade. I. Title.
HF3226.5.H45 1998
382'.30971073—ddc21 98-25400
CIP

9 8 7 6 5 4 3 2 1

The paper used in this publication meets the minimum requirements of
American National Standard for Information Sciences—Permanence of Paper
for Printed Library Materials, ANSI Z39.48-1984

Typeset in Plantin

Composition by Princeton Editorial Associates
Princeton, New Jersey, and Scottsdale, Arizona

Printed by R. R. Donnelley and Sons
Harrisonburg, Virginia

⟨B THE BROOKINGS INSTITUTION

The Brookings Institution is an independent organization devoted to nonpartisan research, education, and publication in economics, government, foreign policy, and the social sciences generally. Its principal purposes are to aid in the development of sound public policies and to promote public understanding of issues of national importance.

The Institution was founded on December 8, 1927, to merge the activities of the Institute for Government Research, founded in 1916, the Institute of Economics, founded in 1922, and the Robert Brookings Graduate School of Economics and Government, founded in 1924.

The Board of Trustees is responsible for the general administration of the Institution, while the immediate direction of the policies, program, and staff is vested in the President, assisted by an advisory committee of the officers and staff. The by-laws of the Institution state: "It is the function of the Trustees to make possible the conduct of scientific research, and publication, under the most favorable conditions, and to safeguard the independence of the research staff in the pursuit of their studies and in the publication of the results of such studies. It is not a part of their function to determine, control, or influence the conduct of particular investigations or the conclusions reached."

The President bears final responsibility for the decision to publish a manuscript as a Brookings book. In reaching his judgment on the competence, accuracy, and objectivity of each study, the President is advised by the director of the appropriate research program and weighs the views of a panel of expert outside readers who report to him in confidence on the quality of the work. Publication of a work signifies that it is deemed a competent treatment worthy of public consideration but does not imply endorsement of conclusions or recommendations.

The Institution maintains its position of neutrality on issues of public policy in order to safeguard the intellectual freedom of the staff. Hence interpretations or conclusions in Brookings publications should be understood to be solely those of the authors and should not be attributed to the Institution, to its trustees, officers, or other staff members, or to the organizations that support its research.

Board of Trustees
James A. Johnson
Chairman

Leonard Abramson
Michael H. Armacost
Elizabeth E. Bailey
Zoë Baird
Alan M. Dachs
Kenneth W. Dam
D. Ronald Daniel
Robert A. Day
Bart Friedman

Stephen Friedman
Henry Louis Gates, Jr.
Teresa Heinz
Samuel Hellman, M.D.
Robert A. Helman
Ann Dibble Jordan
Breene M. Kerr
Thomas G. Labrecque
Jessica Tuchman Mathews
David O. Maxwell
Constance Berry Newman
Maconda Brown O'Connor

Samuel Pisar
Steven L. Rattner
Rozanne L. Ridgway
Judith Rodin
Warren B. Rudman
Michael P. Schulhof
Robert H. Smith
Joan E. Spero
Vincent J. Trosino
Stephen M. Wolf
John D. Zeglis

Honorary Trustees
Vincent M. Barnett, Jr.
Rex J. Bates
Barton M. Biggs
Louis W. Cabot
Frank T. Cary
A. W. Clausen
John L. Clendenin
William T. Coleman, Jr.
Lloyd N. Cutler
Bruce B. Dayton
Douglas Dillon
Charles W. Duncan, Jr.
Walter Y. Elisha
Robert F. Erburu

Robert D. Haas
Andrew Heiskell
F. Warren Hellman
Roy M. Huffington
Thomas W. Jones
Vernon E. Jordan, Jr.
Nannerl O. Keohane
James T. Lynn
William McC. Martin, Jr.
Donald F. McHenry
Robert S. McNamara
Mary Patterson McPherson
Arjay Miller
Donald S. Perkins

J. Woodward Redmond
Charles W. Robinson
James D. Robinson III
David Rockefeller, Jr.
Howard D. Samuel
B. Francis Saul II
Ralph S. Saul
Henry B. Schacht
Robert Brookings Smith
Morris Tanenbaum
John C. Whitehead
James D. Wolfensohn
Ezra K. Zilkha

Foreword

*I*t is widely believed that globalization has resulted in international economic linkages that are as strong as those within nations. Struck by research results suggesting that this perception is dramatically mistaken, John Helliwell spent three years assessing the evidence. His results, reported in this book, provide perhaps the most systematic measurements yet available of the relative importance of global and national economic ties. The original finding, based on a gravity model of trade flows, was that 1988 trade linkages between Canadian provinces were twenty times as dense as those between Canadian provinces and U.S. states of similar size and distance. Using a much larger and more detailed body of data to expand and explain these findings, the author finds that the Canada-U.S. results are applicable to other countries. Domestic trade intensities are ten times international ones for industrialized countries of the Organization of Economic Co-operation and Development (OECD) and much greater for a sample of developing countries. Finally, he examines evidence relating to price linkages, capital mobility, migration, and knowledge spillovers, finding in all cases extensive border effects.

The evidence presented in this book offers a challenge to economists, policymakers, and citizens alike to explain why national economies have so much staying power and to consider whether this is a good or bad thing. Helliwell argues that since large and small industrial economies have similar levels of income, despite the presence of high border effects, increased globalization offers diminishing returns beyond levels sufficient to permit the ready exploitation of comparative advantage in trade and relatively easy access to knowledge developed elsewhere.

John F. Helliwell is professor of economics at the University of British Columbia. Much of the research and writing of this book were carried out during 1995–96, when the author was visiting Harvard University and the Brookings Institution on the Hong Kong Bank Fulbright Fellowship. He is grateful for this support and hospitality, as well as for research support from the Social Sciences and Humanities Research Council of Canada, which made possible the essential research assistance provided by Jamie Armour, Joel Bruneau, Julie Chu, Andrea Podhorsky, Carlos Rosell, Julianne Young, and Zhihao Yu. Helpful comments were received at many seminar presentations of parts of the research. The author wishes to extend special thanks for the helpful comments or research collaboration of Robert Allen, Michael Anderson, Ralph Bryant, Dick Cooper, Brian Copeland, Don Davis, Erwin Diewert, Barry Eichengreen, Charles Engel, Martin Feldstein, John Flemming, David Green, Marc Gaudry, Keith Head, Wolfgang Keller, John McCallum, Ross McKitrick, Hans Messinger, Mancur Olson, John Ries, John Rogers, Fernando Sanz, Charles Schultze, Linda Tesar, Dan Trefler, Shang-Jin Wei, and Holger Wolf.

Princeton Editorial Associates edited the manuscript and prepared the index. Evelyn M. E. Taylor provided administrative support for the project. Jennifer Eichberger and Helen Kim verified the manuscript.

Funding for the Integrating National Economies project came from the Center for Global Partnership of the Japan Foundation, the Curry Foundation, the Ford Foundation, the Korea Foundation, the Tokyo Club Foundation for Global Studies, the United States-Japan Foundation, the German Marshall Fund of the United States, and the Alex C. Walker Educational and Charitable Foundation. The author and Brookings are grateful for their support.

The views expressed in this book are those of the author and should not be ascribed to the persons or organizations whose assistance is acknowledged or to the trustees, officers, or staff members of the Brookings Institution.

MICHAEL H. ARMACOST
President

June 1998
Washington, D.C.

Contents

Tables

Preface to the Studies on Integrating National Economies

E CONOMIC interdependence among nations has increased sharply in the past half century. For example, while the value of total production of industrial countries increased at a rate of about 9 percent a year on average between 1964 and 1992, the value of the exports of those nations grew at an average rate of 12 percent, and lending and borrowing across national borders through banks surged upward even more rapidly at 23 percent a year. This international economic interdependence has contributed to significantly improved standards of living for most countries. Continuing international economic integration holds out the promise of further benefits. Yet the increasing sensitivity of national economies to events and policies originating abroad creates dilemmas and pitfalls if national policies and international cooperation are poorly managed.

The Brookings Project on Integrating National Economies, of which this study is a component, focuses on the interplay between two fundamental facts about the world at the end of the twentieth century. First, the world will continue for the foreseeable future to be organized politically into nation-states with sovereign governments. Second, increasing economic integration among nations will continue to erode differences among national economies and undermine the autonomy of national governments. The project explores the opportunities and tensions arising from these two facts.

Scholars from a variety of disciplines have produced twenty-one studies for the first phase of the project. Each study examines the heightened competition between national political sovereignty and

increased cross-border economic integration. This preface iden-
tifies background themes and issues common to all the studies and
provides a brief overview of the project as a whole.[1]

Increasing World Economic Integration

Two underlying sets of causes have led nations to become more
closely intertwined. First, technological, social, and cultural changes
have sharply reduced the effective economic distances among nations. Second, many of the government policies that traditionally
inhibited cross-border transactions have been relaxed or even
dismantled.

The same improvements in transportation and communications
technology that make it much easier and cheaper for companies in
New York to ship goods to California, for residents of Strasbourg
to visit relatives in Marseilles, and for investors in Hokkaido to buy
and sell shares on the Tokyo Stock Exchange facilitate trade,
migration, and capital movements spanning nations and con-
tinents. The sharply reduced costs of moving goods, money,
people, and information underlie the profound economic truth
that technology has made the world markedly smaller.

New communications technology has been especially significant
for financial activity. Computers, switching devices, and telecom-
munications satellites have slashed the cost of transmitting information internationally, of confirming transactions, and of paying for
transactions. In the 1950s, for example, foreign exchange could be
bought and sold only during conventional business hours in the
initiating party's time zone. Such transactions can now be carried out
instantaneously twenty-four hours a day. Large banks pass the
management of their worldwide foreign-exchange positions around
the globe from one branch to another, staying continuously ahead of
the setting sun.

Such technological innovations have increased the knowledge of
potentially profitable international exchanges and of economic op-

---

1. A complete list of authors and study titles is included at the beginning of this volume,
facing the title page.

portunities abroad. Those developments, in turn, have changed consumers' and producers' tastes. Foreign goods, foreign vacations, foreign financial investments—virtually anything from other nations—have lost some of their exotic character.

Although technological change permits increased contact among nations, it would not have produced such dramatic effects if it had been countermanded by government policies. Governments have traditionally taxed goods moving in international trade, directly restricted imports and subsidized exports, and tried to limit international capital movements. Those policies erected "separation fences" at the borders of nations. From the perspective of private sector agents, separation fences imposed extra costs on cross-border transactions. They reduced trade and, in some cases, eliminated it. During the 1930s governments used such policies with particular zeal, a practice now believed to have deepened and lengthened the Great Depression.

After World War II, most national governments began—sometimes unilaterally, more often collaboratively—to lower their separation fences, to make them more permeable, or sometimes even to tear down parts of them. The multilateral negotiations under the auspices of the General Agreement on Tariffs and Trade (GATT)—for example, the Kennedy Round in the 1960s, the Tokyo Round in the 1970s, and most recently the protracted negotiations of the Uruguay Round, formally signed only in April 1994—stand out as the most prominent examples of fence lowering for trade in goods. Though contentious and marked by many compromises, the GATT negotiations are responsible for sharp reductions in at-the-border restrictions on trade in goods and services. After the mid-1980s a large number of developing countries moved unilaterally to reduce border barriers and to pursue outwardly oriented policies.

The lowering of fences for financial transactions began later and was less dramatic. Nonetheless, by the 1990s government restrictions on capital flows, especially among the industrial countries, were much less important and widespread than at the end of World War II and in the 1950s.

By shrinking the economic distances among nations, changes in technology would have progressively integrated the world economy even in the absence of reductions in governments' separation fences. Reductions in separation fences would have enhanced interdependence even without the technological innovations. Together, these two sets of evolutionary changes have reinforced each other and strikingly transformed the world economy.

Changes in the Government of Nations

Simultaneously with the transformation of the global economy, major changes have occurred in the world's political structure. First, the number of governmental decisionmaking units in the world has expanded markedly, and political power has been diffused more broadly among them. Rising nationalism and, in some areas, heightened ethnic tensions have accompanied that increasing political pluralism.

The history of membership in international organizations documents the sharp growth in the number of independent states. For example, only 44 nations participated in the Bretton Woods conference of July 1944, which gave birth to the International Monetary Fund. But by the end of 1970, the IMF had 118 member nations. The number of members grew to 150 by the mid-1980s and to 178 by December 1993. Much of this growth reflects the collapse of colonial empires. Although many nations today are small and carry little individual weight in the global economy, their combined influence is considerable, and their interests cannot be ignored as easily as they were in the past.

A second political trend, less visible but equally important, has been the gradual loss of the political and economic hegemony of the United States. Immediately after World War II, the United States by itself accounted for more than one-third of world production. By the early 1990s the U.S. share had fallen to about one-fifth. Concurrently, the political and economic influence of the European colonial powers continued to wane, and the economic significance of nations outside Europe and North America, such as Japan, Korea, Indonesia, China, Brazil, and Mexico, increased. A world in which economic power and influence are widely diffused has displaced a world in which one or a few nations effectively dominated international decisionmaking.

Turmoil and the prospect of fundamental change in the former-ly centrally planned economies compose a third factor causing radical changes in world politics. During the era of central plan-ning, governments in those nations tried to limit external influen-ces on their economies. Now leaders in the formerly planned economies are trying to adopt reforms modeled on Western capitalist principles. To the extent that these efforts succeed, those nations will increase their economic involvement with the rest of the world. Political and economic alignments among the Western industrialized nations will be forced to adapt.

Governments and scholars have begun to assess these three trends, but their far-reaching ramifications will not be clear for decades.

Dilemmas for National Policies

Cross-border economic integration and national political sovereignty have increasingly come into conflict, leading to a grow-ing mismatch between the economic and political structures of the world. The effective domains of economic markets have come to coincide less and less with national governmental jurisdictions.

When the separation fences at nations' borders were high, governments and citizens could sharply distinguish "internation-al" from "domestic" policies. International policies dealt with at-the-border barriers, such as tariffs and quotas, or responded to events occurring abroad. In contrast, domestic policies were con-cerned with everything behind the nation's borders, such as com-petition and antitrust rules, corporate governance, product standards, worker safety, regulation and supervision of financial institutions, environmental protection, tax codes, and the government's budget. Domestic policies were regarded as matters about which nations were sovereign, to be determined by the preferences of the nation's citizens and its political institutions, without regard for effects on other nations.

As separation fences have been lowered and technological in-novations have shrunk economic distances, a multitude of formerly neglected differences among nations' domestic policies have become exposed to international scrutiny. National governments and international negotiations must thus increasingly deal with "deeper"—behind-the-border—integration. For example, if country A permits companies to emit air and water pollutants whereas country B does not, companies that use pollution-generating methods of production will find it cheaper to produce in country A. Companies in country B that compete internationally with companies in country A are likely to complain that foreign competitors enjoy unfair advantages and to press for international pollution standards.

Deeper integration requires analysis of the economic and the political aspects of virtually all nonborder policies and practices. Such issues have already figured prominently in negotiations over the evolution of the European Community, over the Uruguay Round of GATT negotiations, over the North American Free Trade Agreement (NAFTA), and over the bilateral economic relationships between Japan and the United States. Future debates about behind-the-border policies will occur with increasing frequency and prove at least as complex and contentious as the past negotiations regarding at-the-border restrictions.

Tensions about deeper integration arise from three broad sources: cross-border spillovers, diminished national autonomy, and challenges to political sovereignty.

Cross-Border Spillovers

Some activities in one nation produce consequences that spill across borders and affect other nations. Illustrations of these spillovers abound. Given the impact of modern technology of banking and securities markets in creating interconnected networks, lax rules in one nation erode the ability of all other nations to enforce banking and securities rules and to deal with fraudulent transactions. Given the rapid diffusion of knowledge, science and technology policies in one nation generate knowledge that other nations can use without full payment. Labor market policies become matters of concern to other nations because workers migrate in search of work; policies in one nation can trigger migration that floods or starves labor markets elsewhere. When one nation dumps pollutants into the air or water that other nations breathe or drink, the matter goes beyond the unitary concern of the polluting nation and becomes a matter for international negotiation. Indeed, the hydrocarbons that are emitted into the atmosphere when individual nations burn coal for generating electricity contribute to global warming and are thereby a matter of concern for the entire world.

The tensions associated with cross-border spillovers can be especially vexing when national policies generate outcomes alleged to be competitively inequitable, as in the example in which country A permits companies to emit pollutants and country B does not. Or consider a situation in which country C requires commodities, whether produced at home or abroad, to meet certain design standards, justified for safety reasons. Foreign competitors may find it too expensive to meet these standards. In that event, the standards in C act very much like tariffs or quotas, effectively narrowing or even eliminating foreign competition for domestic producers. Citing examples of this sort, producers or governments in individual nations often complain that business is not conducted on a "level playing field." Typically, the complaining nation proposes that *other* nations adjust their policies to moderate or remove the competitive inequities.

Arguments for creating a level playing field are troublesome at best. International trade occurs precisely because of differences among nations—in resource endowments, labor skills, and consumer tastes. Nations specialize in producing goods and services in which they are relatively most efficient. In a fundamental sense, cross-border trade is valuable because the playing field is *not* level.

When David Ricardo first developed the theory of comparative advantage, he focused on differences among nations owing to climate or technology. But Ricardo could as easily have ascribed the productive differences to differing "social climates" as to physical or technological climates. Taking all "climatic" differences as given, the theory of comparative advantage argues that free trade among nations will maximize global welfare.

Taken to its logical extreme, the notion of leveling the playing field implies that nations should become homogeneous in all major respects. But that recommendation is unrealistic and even pernicious. Suppose country A decides that it is too poor to afford the costs of a clean environment, and will thus permit the production of goods that pollute local air and water supplies. Or suppose it concludes that it cannot afford stringent protections for worker safety. Country A will then argue that it is inappropriate for other nations to impute to country A the value they themselves place on a clean environment and safety standards (just as it would be inappropriate to impute the A valuations to the environment of other nations). The core of the idea of political sovereignty is to permit national residents to order their lives and property in accord with their own preferences.

Which perspective about differences among nations in behind-the-border policies is more compelling? Is country A merely exercising its national preferences and appropriately exploiting its comparative advantage in goods that are dirty or dangerous to produce? Or does a legitimate international problem exist that justifies pressure from other nations urging country A to accept changes in its policies (thus curbing its national sovereignty)? When national governments negotiate resolutions to such questions—trying to agree whether individual nations are legitimately exercising sovereign choices or, alternatively, engaging in behavior that is unfair or damaging to other nations—the dialogue is invariably contentious because the resolutions depend on the typically complex circumstances of the international spillovers and on the relative weights accorded to the interests of particular individuals and particular nations.

Diminished National Autonomy

As cross-border economic integration increases, governments experience greater difficulties in trying to control events within their borders. Those difficulties, summarized by the term *diminished autonomy,* are the second set of reasons why tensions arise from the competition between political sovereignty and economic integration.

For example, nations adjust monetary and fiscal policies to influence domestic inflation and employment. In setting these policies, smaller countries have always been somewhat constrained by foreign economic events and policies. Today, however, all nations are constrained, often severely. More than in the past, therefore, nations may be better able to achieve their economic goals if they work together collaboratively in adjusting their macroeconomic policies.

Diminished autonomy and cross-border spillovers can sometimes be allowed to persist without explicit international cooperation to deal with them. States in the United States adopt their own tax systems and set policies for assistance to poor single people without any formal cooperation or limitation. Market pressures operate to force a degree of de facto cooperation. If one state taxes corporations too heavily, it knows business will move elsewhere. (Those familiar with older debates about "fiscal federalism" within the United States and other nations will recognize the similarity between those issues and the emerging international debates about deeper integration of national economies.) Analogously, differences among nations in regulations, standards, policies, institutions, and even social and cultural preferences create economic incentives for a kind of arbitrage that erodes or eliminates the differences. Such pressures involve not only the conventional arbitrage that exploits price differentials (buying at one point in geographic space or time and selling at another) but also shifts in the location of production facilities and in the residence of factors of production.

In many other cases, however, cross-border spillovers, arbitrage pressures, and diminished effectiveness of national policies can produce unwanted consequences. In cases involving what economists call externalities (external economies and diseconomies), national governments may need to cooperate to promote mutual interests. For example, population growth, continued urbanization, and the more intensive exploitation of natural resources generate external diseconomies not only within but across national boundaries. External economies generated when benefits spill across national jurisdictions probably also increase in importance (for instance, the gains from basic research and from control of communicable diseases).

None of these situations is new, but technological change and the reduction of tariffs and quotas heighten their importance. When one nation produces goods (such as scientific research) or "bads" (such as pollution) that significantly affect other nations, individual governments acting sequentially and noncooperatively cannot deal effectively with the resulting issues. In the absence of explicit cooperation and political leadership, too few collective goods and too many collective bads will be supplied.

Challenges to Political Sovereignty

The pressures from cross-border economic integration sometimes even lead individuals or governments to challenge the core assumptions of national political sovereignty. Such challenges are a third source of tensions about deeper integration.

The existing world system of nation-states assumes that a nation's residents are free to follow their own values and to select their own political arrangements without interference from others. Similarly, property rights are allocated by nation. (The so-called global commons, such as outer space and the deep seabed, are the sole exceptions.) A nation is assumed to have the sovereign right to exploit its property in accordance with its own preferences and policies. Political sovereignty is thus analogous to the concept of consumer sovereignty (the presumption that the individual consumer best knows his or her own interests and should exercise them freely).

In times of war, some nations have had sovereignty wrested from them by force. In earlier eras, a handful of individuals or groups have questioned the premises of political sovereignty. With the profound increases in economic integration in recent decades, however, a larger number of individuals and groups—and occasionally even their national governments—have identified circumstances in which, it is claimed, some universal or international set of values should take precedence over the preferences or policies of particular nations.

Some groups seize on human-rights issues, for example, or what they deem to be egregiously inappropriate political arrangements in other nations. An especially prominent case occurred when citizens in many nations labeled the former apartheid policies of South Africa an affront to universal values and emphasized that the South African government was not legitimately representing the interests of a majority of South Africa's residents. Such views caused many national governments to apply economic sanctions against South Africa. Examples of value conflicts are not restricted to human rights, however. Groups focusing on environmental issues characterize tropical rain forests as the lungs of the world and the genetic repository for numerous species of plants and animals that are the heritage of all mankind. Such views lead Europeans, North Americans, or Japanese to challenge the timber-cutting policies of Brazilians and Indonesians. A recent controversy over tuna fishing with long drift nets that kill porpoises is yet another example. Environmentalists in the United States whose sensibilities were offended by the drowning of porpoises required U.S. boats at some additional expense to amend their fishing practices. The U.S. fishermen, complaining about imported tuna caught with less regard for porpoises, persuaded the U.S. government to ban such tuna imports (both direct imports from the countries in which the tuna is caught and indirect imports shipped via third countries). Mexico and Venezuela were the main countries affected by this ban; a GATT dispute panel sided with Mexico against the United States in the controversy, which further upset the U.S. environmental community.

A common feature of all such examples is the existence, real or alleged, of "psychological externalities" or "political failures." Those holding such views reject untrammeled political sovereignty for nation-states in deference to universal or non-national values. They wish to constrain the exercise of individual nations' sovereignties through international negotiations or, if necessary, by even stronger intervention.

The Management of International Convergence

In areas in which arbitrage pressures and cross-border spillovers are weak and psychological or political externalities are largely absent, national governments may encounter few problems with deeper integration. Diversity across nations may persist quite easily. But at the other extreme, arbitrage and spillovers in some areas may be so strong that they threaten to erode national diversity completely. Or psychological and political sensitivities may be asserted too powerfully to be ignored. Governments will then be confronted with serious tensions, and national policies and behaviors may eventually converge to common, worldwide patterns (for example, subject to internationally agreed norms or minimum standards). Eventual convergence across nations, if it occurs, could happen in a harmful way (national policies and practices being driven to a least common denominator with externalities ignored, in effect a "race to the bottom") or it could occur with mutually beneficial results ("survival of the fittest and the best").

Each study in this series addresses basic questions about the management of international convergence: if, when, and how national governments should intervene to try to influence the consequences of arbitrage pressures, cross-border spillovers, diminished autonomy, and the assertion of psychological or political externalities. A wide variety of responses is conceivable. We identify six, which should be regarded not as distinct categories but as ranges along a continuum.

National autonomy defines a situation at one end of the continuum in which national governments make decentralized decisions with little or no consultation and no explicit cooperation. This response represents political sovereignty at its strongest, undiluted by any international management of convergence.

Mutual recognition, like national autonomy, presumes decentralized decisions by national governments and relies on market competition to guide the process of international convergence. Mutual recognition, however, entails exchanges of information and consultations among governments to constrain the formation of national regulations and policies. As understood in discussions of economic integration within the European Community, moreover, mutual recognition entails an explicit acceptance by each member nation of the regulations, standards, and certification procedures of other members. For example, mutual recognition allows wine or liquor produced in any European Union country to be sold in all twelve member countries even if production standards in member countries differ. Doctors licensed in France are permitted to practice in

Germany, and vice versa, even if licensing procedures in the two countries differ.

Governments may agree on rules that restrict their freedom to set policy or that promote gradual convergence in the structure of policy. As international consultations and monitoring of compliance with such rules become more important, this situation can be described as *monitored decentralization*. The Group of Seven finance ministers meetings, supplemented by the IMF's surveillance over exchange rate and macroeconomic policies, illustrate this approach to management.

Coordination goes further than mutual recognition and monitored decentralization in acknowledging convergence pressures. It is also more ambitious in promoting intergovernmental cooperation to deal with them. Coordination involves jointly designed mutual adjustments of national policies. In clear-cut cases of coordination, bargaining occurs and governments agree to behave differently from the ways they would have behaved without the agreement. Examples include the World Health Organization's procedures for controlling communicable diseases and the 1987 Montreal Protocol (to a 1985 framework convention) for the protection of stratospheric ozone by reducing emissions of chlorofluorocarbons.

Explicit harmonization, which requires still higher levels of intergovernmental cooperation, may require agreement on regional standards or world standards. Explicit harmonization typically entails still greater departures from decentralization in decisionmaking and still further strengthening of international institutions. The 1988 agreement among major central banks to set minimum standards for the required capital positions of commercial banks (reached through the Committee on Banking Regulations and Supervisory Practices at the Bank for International Settlements) is an example of partially harmonized regulations.

At the opposite end of the spectrum from national autonomy lies *federalist mutual governance*, which implies continuous bargaining and joint, centralized decisionmaking. To make federalist mutual governance work would require greatly strengthened supranational institutions. This end of the management spectrum, now relevant only as an analytical benchmark, is a possible out-come that can be imagined for the middle or late decades of the twenty-first century, possibly even sooner for regional groupings like the European Union.

Overview of the Brookings Project

Despite their growing importance, the issues of deeper economic integration and its competition with national political sovereignty were largely neglected in the 1980s. In 1992 the Brookings Institution initiated its project on Integrating National Economies to direct attention to these important questions.

In studying this topic, Brookings sought and received the cooperation of some of the world's leading economists, political scientists, foreign-policy specialists, and government officials, representing all regions of the world. Although some functional areas require a special focus on European, Japanese, and North American perspectives, at all junctures the goal was to include, in addition, the perspectives of developing nations and the formerly centrally planned economies.

The first phase of the project commissioned the twenty-one scholarly studies listed at the beginning of the book. One or two lead discussants, typically residents of parts of the world other than the area where the author resides, were asked to comment on each study.

Authors enjoyed substantial freedom to design their individual studies, taking due account of the overall themes and goals of the project. The guidelines for the studies requested that at least some of the analysis be carried out with a non-normative perspective. In effect, authors were asked to develop a "baseline" of what might happen in the absence of changed policies or further international cooperation. For their normative analyses, authors were asked to start with an agnostic posture that did not prejudge the net benefits or costs resulting from integration. The project organizers themselves had no presumption about whether national diversity is better or worse than international convergence or about what the individual studies should conclude regarding the desirability of increased integration. On the contrary, each author was asked to address the trade-offs in his or her issue area between diversity and convergence and to locate the area, currently and prospectively, on the spectrum of international management possibilities running between national autonomy through mutual recognition to co-ordination and explicit harmonization.

HENRY J. AARON   SUSAN M. COLLINS
RALPH C. BRYANT   ROBERT Z. LAWRENCE

How Much Do
National Borders
Matter?

Chapter I

Introduction

THIS BOOK attempts to bridge an apparently vast gulf between what is assumed and what is known about the relative tightness of national and international economic linkages. Many well-documented trends show increasing globalization of economic activities, fueled by a series of technological advances from the steamship to the jet plane, from the telegraph to the Internet, and from the printing press to the laser printer. In the light of these changes, it has become common to hear that the national economy has no salience, that the day of the economic nation-state is past, and that global markets are the ones that matter. Underlying these views is a presumption that international economic linkages have intensified to the point that they are as tight as those within national economies, after taking due account of the remaining costs of distance.

Is this presumption correct? So far, almost no evidence has been brought to bear on this question. In the absence of evidence, it has been common, and even understandable, to treat the trends toward globalization as signals that full globalization has already arrived, or will soon do so. What is needed, either to correct or to corroborate this inference, are studies of the levels and changes of the relative tightness of national and international economic ties. This introduction explains some of the reasons for this lack of attention, and then maps a research plan with which to examine the relative importance of national and global economic linkages.

The process of international integration of national economies has been under way, at variable rates and with some reversals, for as long as there have been national economies. In the past fifty years, there have been large increases in the number of national economies and in the extent to which they are economically linked to each other. It has been almost a constant of postwar economic life that international trade has grown faster than national output for most countries and for the world as a whole. The underlying trends are well known and have been widely discussed. The corresponding developments in the structure and intensity of economic relations within nation-states have been much less carefully measured, and are far less widely seen and discussed. Hence, any judgments about the relative tightness of the national and international economies have not had a secure empirical basis.

As noted in the preface to the Brookings series on Integrating National Economies, the increasing intensity of international economic linkages has been driven both by technology and by policy changes. These two types of change are likely to have differing effects on domestic and international economic ties. Declining costs of transport and communication reduce the economic distance between communities, whether or not the communities are in the same country. These cost reductions are likely to strengthen both domestic and international economic linkages. The major effect of policy changes in the past fifty years, however, has been to reduce barriers to international trade erected over the preceding thirty years during the course of two world wars and one global depression.

An inference is frequently made, based on recent increases in international integration, that the intensity of international linkages is approaching, or has even reached, that of internal linkages. This book assesses the evidence for and against this conclusion. To find out to what degree globalization has lessened the relative importance of national borders, it is necessary first to measure the relative strength of internal and external linkages for some base period, and then to track preceding and subsequent changes. This is a tough job, since the established national accounts that make it relatively easy to plot the level and growth of international trade have no counterparts for measuring trade within most national economies. There are some exceptions, mainly for countries with federal or other governmental structures that provide substantial regional autonomy and more incentives for the collection of regional statistics.

The initial and primary focus of this study is on trade flows, starting with some striking results based on data comparing trade flows among Canadian provinces with those between Canadian provinces and individual U.S. states. The original study by McCallum used a gravity model comparing 1988 bilateral merchandise trade between pairs of Canadian provinces with bilateral trade between each of these provinces and the thirty U.S. states with the greatest trade linkages to Canada.[1] He found, after adjusting for differences in size and distance, that interprovincial trade flows were more than twenty times as large as those between provinces and states. Subsequent papers extended the data sample to include 1988 through 1990 and found that even for Quebec the national trade linkages were twenty or more times tighter than those with U.S. states.[2] These papers contrasted these results with survey evidence showing that trade experts, students of economics, and others without special training in economics generally thought that trade linkages were at least as tight between provinces and states as among provinces. The strong statistical support for the gravity model results, coupled with their surprising nature, demanded further efforts to assess their reliability, generality, causes, and consequences. This book documents such further efforts.

Chapter 2 first uses new and revised data to extend the total merchandise trade results to cover the whole period from 1988 through 1996. As expected, the post-1990 increases in bilateral trade between Canada and the United States have been responsible for a drop in the border effects, from about 19 in 1990 (using revised data) to about 12 in 1993 and beyond. That is, even after accounting for the expansion of trade between the United States

---

1. See McCallum (1995).
2. See Helliwell (1996b); Helliwell and McCallum (1995).

and Canada in the wake of the Free Trade Agreement that came into force in 1989, interprovincial trade linkages are still twelve times tighter than those between provinces and states. These results are then split by province, by year, and by direction of trade. Data for 1990 are then used to estimate separate border effects for each of twenty-seven manufacturing industries, with special attention paid to transportation equipment. The chapter concludes with an attempt to measure border effects for services, finding them to be between about 30 and 40 over the 1988–96 period, with little evidence of a 1990–93 reduction parallel to that found for merchandise trade.

Chapter 3 extends the analysis to other Organization for Economic Cooperation and Development (OECD) countries, and to those developing countries with suitable data. In no cases are the data as good as those used in chapter 2, since other countries do not collect statistics for bilateral trade among their constituent states or regions. To make a stab at the problem, input-output data are used to provide estimates of total domestic sales of merchandise, and guesses are made about the average length of internal trade distances. Following these procedures to generate data for internal trade and trade distances, and using International Monetary Fund data for bilateral trade among countries, gravity models are estimated. Internal trade densities *within* typical OECD countries are estimated to be ten times tighter than those *among* the OECD countries, while internal trade densities within European Union (EU) countries are estimated to be more than six times tighter than those among the EU countries. Having a common language is also found to have a significant effect on bilateral trade flows, and border effects are found to fall as gross domestic product (GDP) per capita rises. The global sample of data shows even higher border effects, especially for the developing countries, with differences in per capita GDP being the key to explaining the differences among countries in the size of their border effects.

If border effects in merchandise trade are as large and pervasive as the evidence in chapters 2 and 3 suggests, then they should have counterparts in prices and capital mobility. Chapter 4 surveys the evidence on this score and extends it by comparing capital mobility among provinces with that among countries. For both prices and capital mobility, the evidence appears to support the findings for merchandise trade.

Chapter 5 extends the scope of the study to include population mobility, comparing migration among Canadian provinces and among U.S. states with that from one country to the other. It is no surprise to find that border effects of migration are large, since it is common to assume that goods, services, and capital are freely traded, while population is usually taken to be tied to the nation-state. The evidence for Canada shows that interprovincial migration is almost one hundred times more likely, after adjusting for income differences, population sizes, and distances, than is migration from the United States to Canada. The border effects for southbound migration are much smaller, reflecting that inter-provincial migration is if anything greater than interstate migration, and revealing also the net migration between the two countries over the past decades.

Chapter 6 surveys the empirical growth literature in search of implications of and for border effects. In so doing, it sets the stage for later speculation about the likely reasons for and consequences of border effects. One key piece of evidence from chapter 6 is that at least some degree of openness appears to assist developing countries to start a process of convergence toward the levels of productivity and per capita incomes in the richer industrial countries. A second result, based on recent research on domestic and international spillovers from research and development, suggests that border effects are if anything higher for knowledge spillovers than for goods and services.

Chapter 7 assesses the overall evidence and outlines the implications for future research and for national and international economic policies. First, an attempt is made to assess trends and likely future levels of border effects. Next some evaluation is made of their consequences. Are border effects good or bad? Do they help to match producers and markets in an efficient way, or do they prevent beneficial exchanges from happening? Perhaps, alternatively, a longer-run equilibrium may be determined by offsetting costs and benefits of border effects. Such an equilibrium might be characterized by sufficiently low border effects to permit useful

international transfers of knowledge and to obtain the main benefits of comparative advantage trade, while still having producers
concentrating mainly on responding to the preferences and values
of their domestic consumers and reaping the transactions cost advantages of operating within known norms and communities.

Chapter 2

Comparing Interprovincial and Province-State Trade

*T*HE BEST evidence so far available about the relative strength of domestic and international trade linkages relates to merchandise trade flows among Canadian provinces and between Canadian provinces and U.S. states. Data for trade between Canadian provinces and U.S. states are available from 1988, the year during which the Free Trade Agreement (FTA) was signed between Canada and the United States. Interprovincial trade flows are available from 1984. Data for 1988 interprovincial and province-state trade provided the basis for John McCallum's study showing that interprovincial trade was more than twenty times larger than trade between provinces and states, after using a gravity model to account for the effects of differences in economic size and geographic distance.[1] A subsequent paper, which made use of an extended data sample that included 1989 and 1990, confirmed the results for Quebec as well as for the country as a whole, and showed how dramatically different these results were from professional and public perceptions.[2]

Only at the end of 1996 did data become available for bilateral interprovincial trade for the years 1991 to 1995, with revisions for 1995 and preliminary data for 1996 added in mid-1997. It is thus possible to extend the earlier results through the implementation phase of the U.S.–Canada FTA, which came into force only in

1. See McCallum (1995).
2. See Helliwell (1996b).

1989 and was later extended to become the North American Free Trade Agreement (NAFTA). During the 1990s there have been very large increases in merchandise trade between Canada and the United States. An earlier paper estimated the implications of these north-south trade increases for border effects.[3] It is now possible to be more systematic in this effort, using the newly released data for interprovincial trade flows, coupled with more comparable data for merchandise trade between provinces and states.

This chapter presents the latest estimates of the relative trade intensities among Canadian provinces and between Canadian provinces and U.S. states, followed by a review of the much more fragmentary data on service trade. Chapter 3 presents a parallel body of results making use of international merchandise trade data, first from Organization for Economic Cooperation and Development (OECD) countries, and then from a more global sample adding eleven developing countries to the OECD countries. As will be explained, the international samples include countries that have sufficiently detailed input-output tables to permit the calculation of data for internal sales of goods to match the *Direction of Trade* statistics published by the International Monetary Fund (IMF) for bilateral trade among countries. Both chapters 2 and 3 make use of the gravity model to facilitate the calculation of border effects using data samples based on many trading pairs of unequal size and distance.

The Gravity Model of Trade Flows

The gravity model is used here and elsewhere as a tool for assessing the importance of national borders. It is necessary to have some model that gives geography a key role as a determinant of the density of economic linkages, and yet permits national borders to be additional factors. Without a model that accounts explicitly for the costs of distance, or more precisely for the extent that distance increases the costs of finding, negotiating, and implementing economic transactions, any border effect would get

3. See Helliwell (1996b).

impossibly mixed up with distance. The gravity model has a long and well-established history in the explanation of trade, transportation, migration, and other transactions over space.

The basic form of the gravity model, true to its namesake, is an equation, linear in logarithms, explaining a bilateral linkage by the mass of two bodies and by the distance between them:

$$\ln S_{ij} = \alpha_0 + \alpha_1 \ln M_i + \alpha_2 \ln M_j + \alpha_3 \ln(\text{DIST}_{ij}) + \alpha_4 B + \varepsilon_{ij} \qquad (2\text{-}1)$$

where S_{ij} is some measure of transaction between i and j, with any movement being from i to j, M_i and M_j are the masses of units i and j, DIST_{ij} is the distance between them, B is a variable that takes the value 1.0 for pairs of i and j that possess some characteristic whose importance is to be assessed, and ε_{ij} is a random error term usually taken to be normally distributed. For the trade equations in this section, provincial or state gross domestic product (GDP) is used as the measure of economic mass, while for the migration equations of chapter 5 population is the relevant measure of mass. For the international samples studied in chapter 3, population and GDP per capita are found to have importantly different effects on trade flows, so the equations there treat these two variables separately.[4]

The gravity equation has always been the most empirically successful means of explaining bilateral trade flows, but has met with differing degrees of theoretical respect depending on the extent to which it was seen to have a well-established theoretical

4. The findings of earlier studies varied as to whether population and per capita incomes should have separate influences on the density of trade flows, and on whether to constrain the income elasticities to be equal for the importer and exporter. As noted by Sanso, Cuairan, and Sanz (1993), early applications of the gravity framework, including Aitken (1973), Linnemann (1966), and Sapir (1981), permitted population and aggregate income to have separate effects, and allowed both effects to have different values for the exporter and importer. Several subsequent studies, including Bergstrand (1989) and Thoumi (1989), used aggregate income and per capita income separately for both importer and exporter. In log-linear form, these two specifications are equivalent to each other. We use the second specification for the equations in chapter 3. For the province-state trade equations reported in this chapter, we find, as did McCallum (1995), that per capita incomes have no systematic effect, so the basic equation includes only aggregate GDPs for the importing and exporting jurisdictions. For the OECD and global samples, where there is a larger variation of per capita incomes, we find that per capita incomes matter, and also that they influence the size of the border effects.

foundation. Despite its use in many early studies of international trade,[5] the equation was considered suspect in that it could not easily be shown to be consistent with the dominant Heckscher-Ohlin model explaining net trade flows in terms of differential factor endowments. Anderson showed that the gravity model could be derived from expenditure share equations assuming commodities to be distinguished by place of production.[6] Anderson also showed that the model should, to be fully consistent with the generalized expenditure share model, include remoteness measures in bilateral share equations, as we do here.[7] Helpman and Bergstrand showed that the gravity model can also be derived from models of trade in differentiated products.[8] Such trade must lie at the core of much of manufacturing trade, given the very large two-way flows of trade in even the most finely disaggregated industry data. Finally, Deardorff showed that a suitable modeling of transport costs produces the gravity equation as an estimation form even for the Heckscher-Ohlin model.[9]

Thus the gravity model has gone from being a theoretical orphan to being the favored child of all main theories of international trade. This makes it a solid tool for the evaluation of border effects, even if it cannot easily be used to discriminate among competing theories of international trade. However, if border effects should continue to be found in national and global samples of data, this will provide strong encouragement for theoretical models that distinguish goods by country of production.

For all of the trade equations, we recognize that the bilateral trade flows being modeled are segments of a larger multilateral system of trading relations. In principle, within a generalized gravity model, each bilateral flow should depend not just on the economic

5. For examples see Linnemann (1966); Pöyhönen (1963); Pulliainen (1963).

6. See Anderson (1979). The distinction of goods by place of production is central to the standard Mundell-Fleming open-economy macroeconomic framework, and has been adopted by many other studies, including Armington (1969), Harrigan (1996), Isard (1977), Trefler (1995), and Wei (1996). In such models, border effects can be due to preferences for home-produced goods over otherwise similar foreign-produced goods.

7. See Anderson (1979).

8. See Bergstrand (1985, 1989); Helpman (1984).

9. See Deardorff (1998).

masses of the two trading parties and the distance separating them, but also on the economic masses and distances of alternative trading partners. To achieve this, we adopt a measure of the economic remoteness of alternative trading partners that is consistent with the earlier migration models of Feder and with the theoretical derivation of Wei.[10] The version employed in an earlier study had one value for each year and country,[11] taking the following form for country j in year t:

$$REM_{jt} = \Sigma_i(DIST_{ij}/GDP_{it}) \qquad (2\text{-}2)$$

where the summation is over all of country j's trading partners. As required by the theory of the gravity model, this measure of the remoteness of alternative markets depends positively on their distance from the domestic market and negatively on their size.[12] There is one respect in which it could be improved and that improvement has now been made, although the effect on the results is minimal. Equation (2-2) gives a single remoteness measure for each country, but in principle it should be different for each partner under consideration, since the variable is supposed to represent the trading opportunities available to j with countries other than i. This can be done by simply removing country i's data from the calculations. The result is a new series that takes a different value to match each bilateral trade relation. It can be expressed as follows, where the remoteness measure is for country j, applicable to trade with country i. The summation now covers all of j's n trading partners excluding i:

$$REM_{jit} = \Sigma_{n,n\neq i}(DIST_{ij}/GDP_{it}) \qquad (2\text{-}3)$$

The above measure of remoteness has been used in the latest results shown in the rest of this chapter and for the OECD and global samples in chapter 3.

10. See Feder (1980); Wei (1996).

11. See Helliwell (1997).

12. It is thus the inverse of Feder's (1980) measure of the attractiveness of alternative markets, and the parallel of Wei's (1996) remoteness measure with σ equal to 1.0. Tests show σ = 1.0 to provide a better-fitting measure of remoteness than any of the higher values considered by Wei.

Aggregate Estimates of Border Effects

In this section we start by presenting the latest estimates for national border effects based on the gravity model applied to data for province-state and interprovincial trade flows. Since there are no comparable measures of trade flows among U.S. states, the data sample used includes all trade flows between the thirty most important trading states and each of the ten Canadian provinces, plus all trade flows among the ten provinces. Some gravity models treat the sum of two-way bilateral trade as the dependent variable.[13] However, we wish here to consider the possibility that border effects may differ between inbound and outbound flows, and in any event we want as large a sample as feasible. Thus we treat exports from i to j separately from exports from j to i. The total sample is thus in principle equal to six hundred observations for trade between provinces and states ($10 \times 30 \times 2$) and one hundred observations for trade among provinces (10×10). These one hundred observations for interprovincial trade are reduced to ninety in those cases where the sample does not include sales within the same province. Also, we exclude all trade pairs with bilateral trade observations of zero in any of the sample years. This means that there are slightly fewer annual observations in the current sample than in earlier work based on data from fewer years. However, the observations omitted relate to very small trade flows, and in any event it is desirable to have an identical sample in each year to enable more precise tests of changes over time in the size of border effects.

For the equations relating to trade among provinces, and between provinces and states, the border variable (here named "HOME," to reflect its role in measuring preference for trading in home country markets) is assigned the value of 1.0 for all trade flows among Canadian provinces. The basic equation estimated, after allowing for the effects of each country's remoteness from alternative trading partners, is thus

$$\ln Sxm = \alpha_0 + \alpha_1 \ln GDPx + \alpha_2 \ln GDPm + \alpha_3 \ln(DISTxm)$$
$$+ \alpha_4 HOME + \alpha_5 \ln REMx + \alpha_6 \ln REMm + \varepsilon_{xm} \quad (2\text{-}4)$$

13. See Frankel and Wei (1993).

where the trade flow goes from state or province x to m. The coefficients on the exporter's and importer's GDPs are expected to be positive, the distance coefficient negative, and both remoteness coefficients positive, since each bilateral trading link is expected to be used more intensively the further either partner is from economically important alternative markets. If the border variable takes a zero coefficient, it would imply that trading relations among Canadian provinces are as dense as those between Canadian provinces and U.S. states. If the coefficient is negative, $\alpha_4 < 0$, this would imply that north-south trading flows between Canadian provinces and U.S. states are larger than those among Canadian provinces, after allowing for differences in size and distance. Conversely, a positive coefficient on HOME implies that trade linkages among the provinces are tighter than those between provinces and states, after allowing for economic size, the distance of each of the partners, and their remoteness from alternative trading partners. The antilog of the coefficient on HOME shows the extent of the border effect. It shows typical province-to-province flows as a fraction (or multiple) of typical province-state flows, where the provinces and states are of the same size and are separated by the same distance. A survey of Canadian economists and political scientists showed that the median respondent expected that province-province trade would be 0.8 times as large as province-state trade,[14] implying a negative value for the coefficient on the border variable.[15]

Equations (i)–(iii) of table 2-1 show the results for the gravity equation (2-4) fitted for each of the years 1988, 1989, and 1990, using the data for interprovincial and province-state trade used in the earlier studies by McCallum for 1988 and by Helliwell for 1988–90.[16] Equation (iv) shows the results of estimating the equations for the three years as a system, with all coefficients constrained to be the same in each year.

Equation (v) then re-estimates the 1990 equation making use of new data from Statistics Canada revising the estimates of province-

---

14. See Helliwell (1996b).
15. Since the logarithm of 0.8 is –0.223, the median respondent implicitly expected the coefficient on HOME to take a coefficient of this value.
16. See Helliwell (1996b); McCallum (1995).

Table 2-1. *Canadian Border Effects, 1988–90*

	Equation				
	(i)	(ii)	(iii)	(iv)	(v)
Observations	676	676	676	3 × 676	676
Estimation method	OLS	OLS	OLS	SUR	OLS
Dependent variable	Province-state	Province-state	Province-state	Province-state	Province-state
ln(Sxm)	1988	1989	1990	1988–90	1990
Constant	−3.50	−3.05	−4.30	−3.6, −3.6, −3.7	−3.60
	(5.1)	(4.2)	(5.5)	(5.4, 5.5, 5.6)	(4.9)
ln(GDPx)	1.19	1.19	1.23	1.20	1.24
	(39.5)	(38.0)	(36.7)	(42.1)	(39.1)
ln(GDPm)	1.06	1.03	1.06	1.05	0.94
	(35.4)	(33.5)	(31.9)	(37.3)	(29.9)
ln(DISTxm)	−1.59	−1.62	−1.57	−1.59	−1.46
	(23.4)	(23.0)	(20.7)	(24.7)	(20.4)
HOME	3.03	2.94	3.23	3.07	2.97
	(24.3)	(22.8)	(23.3)	(26.0)	(22.7)
ln(REMx)	0.77	0.70	0.71	0.74	0.67
	(7.1)	(6.3)	(6.0)	(7.2)	(5.9)
ln(REMm)	0.10	0.24	0.33	0.21	0.25
	(0.9)	(2.1)	(2.7)	(2.0)	(2.2)
$\bar{R}^2$	0.818	0.804	0.787	0.82, 0.81, 0.79	0.790
SEE	1.05	1.09	1.17	1.05, 1.09, 1.17[a]	1.11
Border effect	20.7	19.0	25.3	21.6	19.5

Sources: Sources for tables 2-1–2-7 are author's calculations using the following sources:

Interprovincial trade flows from "Interprovincial and International Trade Flows of Goods," Input-Output Division, Statistics Canada.

Province-state flows from "Merchandise Trade—Exports" and "Merchandise Trade—Imports," Statistics Canada.

Provincial GDP from "Provincial Economic Accounts," Statistics Canada.

State GDP from the Survey of Current Business 1981–92. For 1993–96 state GDP is assumed to grow at the same rate as U.S. GDP.

Distance is typically measured from capital to capital, but for some province and state economic centers it is calculated as a geographic average of latitudes and longitudes of major cities using city population weights. Latitudes and longitudes are from Fitzpatrick and Modlin (1986). The U.S. population is from the 1990 census; the Canadian population is from the 1991 census.

Notes: Absolute values of t-statistics are in parentheses. The dependent variable is the natural log of total shipments of goods from province or state x to province or state m, with ln(GDPx) being the log of the exporter's GDP and ln(GDPm) of the importer's GDP. HOME takes the value 1.0 for each observation recording trade from one province to another.

a. P-value of restriction = .020.

state trade to provide a better match, in concept and magnitude, with the interprovincial trade data.[17] Because the new reconciliation, which required a detailed reworking of the trade numbers, only became available in mid-1997, and is so far only available for 1990, the question arises of how to handle the estimation for other years. The advice from Statistics Canada is that the 1990 adjustment factors may fairly safely be assumed to be an improvement on the previous procedure for years after 1990, but not necessarily for years before then, because of changes in some of the disaggregated industry definitions before 1990. Thus the 1988 and 1989 equations will not be re-estimated, except to look for trends in the border effects, while the new adjustment factors will be used for all of our work for 1991 through 1996, pending eventual release of more up-to-date adjustments based on surveys underway in 1997.

What do the results show? Equations (i)–(iv) essentially match the data and results reported elsewhere,[18] and are only slightly different from McCallum's 1988 results, which so piqued my interest on first sight in 1994. The implied border effects, which appear at the bottom of table 2-1, show that interprovincial trade flows in the years 1988–90, using the best data and methods available at the time, were about twenty times as large as those between provinces and states.

Since this number is surprisingly large and contrasts so strongly with preconceptions, it may be useful, even before proceeding to additional results, to illustrate the underpinnings of the statistical estimates. This can be done in two ways. First, it may be useful to look ahead to the second column of table 2-7, which shows inter-

17. The original data had reconciled the input-output data for foreign trade with the province-state trade data by means of a separate adjustment factor for each province, multiplying all province-state trade flows for that province by whatever figure was required to make the totals for the thirty states equal to a number consistent with the interprovincial trade matrix. The revised data follow the same procedure, but separately for each of twenty-seven component industries of manufacturing, employing much finer disaggregation to establish a concordance between the industry categories used in the input-output and international trade accounts. Since the province-state trade flows differ a great deal from one manufacturing sector to another, the result of the new procedure is that there is now a separate adjustment factor for each aggregate 1990 province-state trade flow.

18. See Helliwell (1997, table 1).

provincial merchandise trade as a ratio to international trade, more than three-quarters of which is with the United States. The ratio is almost 0.75 until the end of the 1980s, falling thereafter to about 0.5 in 1993, with slight further reductions thereafter. The fact that total Canadian interprovincial trade is less than total international trade, and that the ratio fell during the years after the introduction of the U.S.–Canada FTA, perhaps represents the base of information supporting the general view that north-south trade linkages are tighter than those among the provinces. What the crude data do not capture, of course, is that the trading potential of U.S. states, in terms of economic size and moderate shipping distances, is vastly greater than that of the Canadian provinces. Hence the fact that total trade with the United States is not much larger than that among provinces should lead to the expectation of a significant border effect. Matched trading pairs or estimated gravity equations are needed to make better estimates of the likely size of the border effects.

Second, it may be helpful to examine actual trade flows for some large and representative pairs of provinces and states, chosen to be of equivalent distance and making due allowance for their differences in size. Looking at some representative trade flows in 1990, the year for which the best current reconciliation of the interprovincial and international trade data exists, it is suitable to start with two of the largest trading pairs: Quebec and Ontario, and Quebec and New York. Quebec shares a border with both New York and Ontario, and New York's 1990 GDP was two and one-half times that of Ontario. A gravity model without border effects would suggest that Quebec would export more than twice as much to New York as to Ontario, while in fact Quebec exported more than five times as much to Ontario as to New York, for a total border effect of approximately 13. A similar pattern is found for Ontario's exports. According to a gravity model without border effects, Ontario would export more than three times as much to New York as to Quebec, while it actually sold more than twice as much to Quebec, for a total relative border effect of 8.1.

Examination of trade between more distant trading partners might help to avoid the possible complications of adjacency. Ontario is almost equidistant from British Columbia, Washington state, and California. In 1990 the Californian economy was almost twelve times larger than that of British Columbia and thus should have provided, without border effects, a market almost twelve times as large. Ontario merchandise shipments to British Columbia were actually almost twice as large as those to California, for a total border effect of 21. Washington GDP was more than one-third larger than that of British Columbia, but Ontario's exports to British Columbia were more than twelve times larger than those to Washington, for a total border effect of 21.

Finally, it would be useful to look at a specially tight cross-border trading relationship—that between Ontario and Michigan. The North American auto industry has been integrated for auto producers since the 1965 Canada–United States Automotive Products Agreement (1965 Auto Pact), and even before then production in the two countries was dominated by the big three auto companies (Ford, General Motors, and Chrysler), each of which operated plants in both countries. Ontario and Michigan are the key centers of the industry, and most Ontario parts and assembly plants are within a short distance of the Michigan plants. In addition, trade between the two countries in autos and parts has grown substantially since 1964, and in 1990 represented almost 10 percent of total merchandise trade between the two countries. Shipments from Ontario to Michigan show the effects of this special relationship. Although the Michigan economy is 50 percent larger than that of Quebec, Ontario shipments to Michigan in 1990 were more than twice as large as those to Quebec, producing a border effect of 0.67 if the average distance were the same between Ontario and Quebec as between Ontario and Michigan. Our measure of distance has the average Ontario-Quebec trading distance 50 percent greater than that between Ontario and Michigan, which would raise the border effect to 1.0, still far below that estimated for typical trading pairs of provinces and states. In the light of this very tight industry-based trade linkage between the two main centers of the North American auto industry, Anderson and Smith were surprised to find a border effect for transportation equipment (primarily autos and parts) even larger than that for total merchandise trade.[19] The key to this puzzle may lie in the fact that the 1965 Auto Pact provided free trade for manufacturers but not for consumers. Thus autos and parts moved freely across the border within the unified production sector, while most other shipments may have been within national boundaries. This hypothesis will be tested later in the chapter, making use of industry-level data.

The purpose of the examples given here is to illustrate the values and variety inherent in the raw data. So far, the examples given all relate to exports from Canada to the United States, in order to provide direct comparison with exports to another province. Anderson and Smith report, as will be shown later in this chapter, that border effects are larger for northbound than for southbound trade, which means that examples chosen solely from southbound trade will underestimate average border effects.[20]

Another way of summarizing the basic data would be to look at average values. On average, the thirty large U.S. states in the sample had total GDPs 2.8 times as large as the average for the ten Canadian provinces. However, average merchandise trade flows from province to province were 3.3 times as large as those from provinces to states. Average distances among provinces are slightly greater (by about seventy miles, or 7 percent) than those between provinces and states. A crude border effect obtained by multiplying 2.8 times 3.3 is just over 9 (9.24). This is smaller than the border effect estimated by the logarithmic gravity model for 1990, but still nine times larger than is generally thought.

The difference between this "back-of-the-envelope" calculation and the larger value obtained from econometric estimation of the gravity model in logarithmic form invites further investigation. The most important difference between the two methods of estimation is that the logarithmic form chooses parameters so as to minimize the sum of squared proportionate errors in the prediction of trade flows, and in the process permits the effects of GDP and distance to have more or less than equal proportionate effects on trade flows. The border effect coefficient is estimated so as to make the mean proportionate error equal zero both for province-province

19. See Anderson and Smith (1996, table 3).
20. See Anderson and Smith (1997).

and province-state trade flows. In contrast, the back-of-the-envelope calculation ignores the effects of distance (or at least assumes them to be independent of other factors, and to have the same total effect on province-province and province-state trade flows), assumes that trade moves proportionately with both exporter and importer GDPs, and chooses the border effect that correctly predicts the ratio of total interprovincial to total province-state trade flows. It is possible to examine which of these assumptions has the most important effects.

Since the logarithmic estimation provides the larger estimate of the border effect, this suggests that border effects may be larger for some of the smaller trade flows, or at least that some large trade flows are being underestimated by the logarithmic form. This can be relatively easily checked by various means. One simple way is to take the predicted values from the logarithmic estimation, convert them into level form, and compute the mean forecast errors separately for the province-province and the province-state trade flows. The results show, as expected, that the mean predicted trade flows between provinces and states exceed the actual values, while the reverse is true for the interprovincial trade flows. This is in contrast to the mean proportionate errors, which are equal to zero for both the province-province and the province-state trade flows, since the border coefficient was estimated to ensure this result.

What lies behind this difference between the proportionate and absolute results? In light of the large size of the Auto Pact–related trade flows between Ontario and Michigan, and of the apparently small size of the back-of-the-envelope border effect for that trading pair, a good starting point would be to see the extent to which the Auto Pact is responsible for the difference. This can be done either by including an Auto Pact variable in the equation, with the value of 1.0 for trade flows between Ontario and Michigan, or simply by excluding those observations from the analysis. In either case, the result is to eliminate the logarithmic model's underprediction of average trade flows between provinces and states. If the Auto Pact variable is included in the equation, it takes a coefficient of 1.23 with a t-value of 1.6, with no change in the estimate of the border effect. The coefficient has the effect of more than doubling the estimated trade flows between Ontario and Michigan, however, and eliminates, on average, two of the largest prediction errors, when measured in millions of dollars of trade. Since these flows loom large in total trade, but represent only 2 observations out of 676 in the estimation, they are responsible for a substantial part of the difference between the back-of-the-envelope and regression estimates of 1990 border effects. This can be seen by repeating the average calculations eliminating the Ontario-Michigan trade flows. Removing just those two observations raises the ratio of average province-province to province-state trade from 3.3 to 4.4, increasing the back-of-the-envelope border calculation from under 10 to 12.3.

Another way of allowing for the fact that border effects are lower for some large trading pairs is to use weighted regression to re-estimate equation (v) of table 2-1. Weighting by size of shipments would not be appropriate, since this would make the weighting depend on the error term. To avoid the spurious correlations this would entail, it is necessary to construct a synthetic measure of the size of the shipments, and then use this as a basis for weighting. If the border effect is unchanged, then the conclusion must be that the border effect does not vary systematically with size. The synthetic measure of trading size used is derived directly from the underlying gravity model, being the product of the importer and exporter GDPs divided by the distance between the trading partners. In logarithmic form, to match the form of the gravity equation, this variable is then used as a weighting factor, thereby giving more importance to the larger trading pathways. The estimated border effect is unchanged, rising insignificantly from 18.92 to 18.95. Thus there appears to be no systematic evidence that Canada–U.S. border effects are either smaller or larger for the larger trading pairs. The logarithmic form of the gravity equation appears not to be driven unduly by the trade flows between smaller trading partners.

One more way of testing the appropriateness of the logarithmic form is to do a Box-Cox estimation of the model. This lets the data choose the best-fitting mix of linear and log-linear estimation. Gaudry and others did this using McCallum's 1988 data sample, while Fernando Sanz did similar tests using the 1988–90 data set. In both cases, the optimal estimation structure was very close to the logarithmic form, and the border effects were also very similar to those in the original published papers.[21] These provide useful robustness checks on the simpler logarithmic form. Since the results are so similar, and are much easier to interpret for the logarithmic form, the latter will be used here.

As already reported, there have been substantial increases in Canada–U.S. trade since the Canada–U.S. FTA came into effect, so that aggregate border effects will have fallen since 1990, as shown by the results reported in table 2-2. To give a rough sample, based on preliminary data, of how the border effect might have been affected, shipments from Ontario to California grew by 85 percent from 1990 to 1995, while those to British Columbia and Washington state both shrank by about 10 percent. As a result, pairwise 1995 Ontario border effects, relative to exports to British Columbia, remained above 20 for Washington and fell to just below 10 for California. More representative estimates of border effects by province, and their trends, are reported in the next section.

Table 2-2 shows more systematic results, based on the full sample of data, for the years 1991 through 1996. The average border effect fell from its 1990 value of 19.5 to about 12 in 1993. It remained on average about 12 for 1993 through 1996, punctuated by a movement up to 14 in 1995. What can be said about the size and significance of the post-FTA movements in the border effect? The question is complicated by the fact that the more precise reconciliation of the interprovincial and international trade data is currently available only for 1990. As shown in table 2-1, the more precise reconciliation has the effect of lowering the 1990 border effect by about 20 percent. In order to guard against too-high estimates of the border effect, the table 2-2 results use the same adjustments for 1991 through 1996, on grounds that they are likely to be better than the previous method.

21. The results of Gaudry, Blum, and McCallum, using the same data as McCallum (1995), are given in Gaudry, Blum, and McCallum (1996). Fernando Sanz used the data from Helliwell (1996b) and the same estimated procedures used by Sanso, Cuairan, and Sanz (1993).

Table 2-2. *Canadian Border Effects, 1991–96*

	Equation					
	i	*ii*	*iii*	*iv*	*v*	*vi*
Observations	676	676	676	676	676	676
Estimation method	OLS	OLS	OLS	OLS	OLS	OLS
Dependent variable	Province-state	Province-state	Province-state	Province-state	Province-state	Province-state
ln(Sxm)	1991	1992	1993	1994	1995	1996
Constant	−3.13	−1.46	−2.70	−1.20	−1.89	−1.28
	(4.2)	(1.8)	(3.5)	(1.4)	(2.1)	(1.5)
ln(GDPx)	1.21	1.12	1.19	1.08	1.11	1.08
	(37.7)	(33.0)	(35.9)	(30.8)	(31.0)	(30.4)
ln(GDPm)	0.91	0.86	0.95	0.90	0.96	0.95
	(28.8)	(25.8)	(29.1)	(25.9)	(27.1)	(26.9)
ln(DISTxm)	−1.43	−1.47	−1.48	−1.46	−1.52	−1.51
	(19.9)	(21.2)	(19.9)	(20.3)	(20.8)	(21.0)
HOME	2.84	2.72	2.51	2.44	2.64	2.48
	(21.4)	(20.6)	(18.4)	(17.8)	(19.0)	(18.0)
ln(REMx)	0.62	0.81	0.54	0.69	0.65	0.66
	(5.5)	(6.4)	(4.6)	(5.3)	(4.8)	(5.0)
ln(REMm)	0.19	0.44	0.22	0.45	0.54	0.59
	(1.7)	(3.5)	(1.9)	(3.5)	(4.0)	(4.5)
$\overline{R}^2$	0.777	0.780	0.764	0.762	0.770	0.768
SEE	1.12	1.11	1.15	1.15	1.17	1.16
Border effect	17.0	15.2	12.3	11.4	14.0	11.9

Notes: Absolute values of t-statistics are in parentheses. The dependent variable is the natural log of total shipments of goods from province or state x to province or state m, with ln(GDPx) being the log of the exporter's GDP and ln(GDPm) of the importer's GDP. HOME takes the value 1.0 for each observation recording trade from one province to another.

The sharp drop in the border effect from 1990 to 1993, coupled with its rough constancy since, suggests that the major adjustments of trade patterns following the FTA may have been completed. As is noted later in the chapter, the first five years after the adoption of the 1965 U.S.–Canada Auto Pact showed large increases in the ratio of trade in cars and parts to total trade, with no major increases thereafter. The parallel between the two cases is by no means exact, as the auto industry on both sides of the border is dominated by the same three large firms, while the effects of the FTA are felt by a much more diverse and less connected set of firms on both sides of the border. For the moment, the parallel nature of the two adjustment paths should be seen as suggestive rather than conclusive.

Border Effects by Year, by Province, and by Direction of Trade

It might be expected that border effects would have different levels and trends from province to province, reflecting large inter-provincial variations in resource endowments, industrial struc-tures, and geography. Table 2-3 uses the gravity model to compare levels and trends in border effects from province to province. The equations cover the nine-year period 1988 to 1996. The gravity model is simplified by constraining the exporter and importer GDP effects to be the same as each other, and from year to year. The same is done for the remoteness effects, while the distance effects are constrained to be the same for each year. All of these coefficients can change from province to province, but not from year to year. All that changes from year to year is the border effect, which thus captures any changes that might apply differently to interprovincial and province-state trade.[22] Shown in the top panel of table 2-3 are results of the restricted model applied to the full data set; the results can be compared with those in table 2-2 to see the impact on the estimates of the national border effects. The equation also adds data for within-province shipments, to permit the estimation of possible provincial border effects.[23] There is some

22. These restrictions are rejected by the data, but are used nonetheless to make it more straightforward to compare border effects from year to year and later to estimate them separately for northbound and southbound trade. Tests show that imposing these restric-tions does not change the average values for the border coefficients.

23. Comparing province-state border results with those calculated for OECD countries in the next chapter requires that account be taken of provincial as well as national border effects, since total domestic shipments include both intraprovincial and interprovincial sales. Wolf (1997) finds more significant evidence of intrastate trading preference using a survey of 1993 U.S. commodity shipments within and among the forty-eight continental states.

Table 2-3. *Border Effects by Province*

Coefficients (t-values)	1988	1989	1990	1991	1992	1993	1994	1995	1996
Canada: ln(DIST) = −1.355 (22.8)									
686 observations ln(GDP) = 1.054 (46.5)									
ln(REM) = 0.195 (4.9)									
OWN = 0.677 (1.8)									
Border coefficient	2.81	2.83	2.92	2.82	2.74	2.49	2.46	2.60	2.47
t-value	(20.8)	(20.1)	(21.6)	(20.7)	(20.2)	(18.1)	(18.0)	(18.8)	(18.0)
R^2		0.780	0.760	0.783	0.772	0.773	0.766	0.764	0.774	0.772
Border effect	16.7	16.9	18.5	16.7	15.6	12.0	11.7	13.5	11.8
Newfoundland: ln(DIST) = −2.034 (4.5)									
72 observations ln(GDP) = 1.047 (8.2)									
ln(REM) = 0.059 (0.0)									
OWN = 1.17 (0.8)									
Border coefficient	2.02	2.39	2.39	2.65	2.38	2.02	1.67	2.69	2.42
t-value	(4.6)	(4.5)	(6.0)	(5.6)	(4.5)	(3.7)	(3.3)	(5.0)	(4.4)
R^2		0.477	0.345	0.549	0.488	0.368	0.379	0.326	0.398	0.418
Border effect	7.5	10.9	10.9	14.1	10.8	7.5	5.3	14.7	11.3
New Brunswick: ln(DIST) = −1.545 (9.0)									
79 observations ln(GDP) = 0.947 (9.6)									
ln(REM) = 0.038 (0.2)									
OWN = −0.235 (0.2)									
Border coefficient	2.69	2.80	2.71	2.65	2.69	2.48	2.38	2.46	2.31
t-value	(8.3)	(7.9)	(6.7)	(7.4)	(7.8)	(7.3)	(6.7)	(7.3)	(6.9)
R^2		0.717	0.695	0.581	0.637	0.694	0.701	0.667	0.691	0.695
Border effect	14.7	16.5	15.1	14.1	14.7	11.9	10.8	11.7	10.0
Nova Scotia: ln(DIST) = −1.458 (8.3)									
79 observations ln(GDP) = 1.178 (13.5)									
ln(REM) = 0.192 (0.7)									
OWN = −0.112 (0.1)									
Border coefficient	3.33	3.29	3.48	3.12	3.05	2.91	3.03	3.15	3.23
t-value	(10.2)	(10.0)	(11.7)	(9.9)	(9.3)	(8.4)	(9.8)	(9.8)	(10.2)
R^2		0.745	0.743	0.793	0.745	0.723	0.704	0.754	0.725	0.747
Border effect	28.0	26.9	32.4	22.7	21.1	18.3	20.7	23.3	25.2

Table 2-3. *(continued)*

	Coefficients (t-values)	1988	1989	1990	1991	1992	1993	1994	1995	1996
Prince Edward Island: 72 observations	ln(DIST) = −1.516 (7.3) ln(GDP) = 0.987 (6.7) ln(REM) = −0.092 (0.4) OWN = 1.568 (1.1)									
Border coefficient		2.87	2.68	3.19	3.0	3.19	2.84	3.03	3.15	2.91
t-value		(6.1)	(5.6)	(6.9)	(6.3)	(7.5)	(6.9)	(6.9)	(7.0)	(7.1)
R^2			0.564	0.518	0.566	0.501	0.607	0.608	0.604	0.605	0.607
Border effect		17.6	14.6	24.2	20.1	24.4	17.1	20.6	23.4	18.4
Quebec: 79 observations	ln(DIST) = −0.964 (12.2) ln(GDP) = 0.913 (18.8) ln(REM) = 0.051 (0.5) OWN = 0.464 (0.9)									
Border coefficient		2.81	2.79	2.95	2.79	2.63	2.33	2.28	2.36	2.27
t-value		(15.5)	(16.6)	(17.1)	(15.9)	(16.2)	(12.6)	(12.8)	(14.1)	(13.3)
R^2			0.850	0.870	0.883	0.870	0.869	0.801	0.821	0.857	0.851
Border effect		16.7	16.3	19.2	16.2	13.9	10.3	9.8	10.6	9.7
Ontario: 79 observations	ln(DIST) = −0.825 (6.9) ln(GDP) = 1.123 (17.3) ln(REM) = −0.070 (0.7) OWN = −0.399 (0.6)									
Border coefficient		3.14	3.18	3.25	3.16	2.96	2.75	2.60	2.52	2.54
t-value		(14.9)	(14.8)	(14.6)	(14.3)	(13.7)	(12.4)	(11.9)	(11.3)	(11.7)
R^2			0.854	0.849	0.841	0.841	0.843	0.830	0.833	0.823	0.828
Border effect		23.0	24.0	25.8	23.7	19.3	15.7	13.5	12.4	12.7
Manitoba: 79 observations	ln(DIST) = −2.14 (15.2) ln(GDP) = 1.062 (19.3) ln(REM) = −0.140 (1.4) OWN = −0.874 (1.3)									
Border coefficient		2.70	2.72	2.88	2.71	2.66	2.24	2.22	2.34	2.18
t-value		(13.0)	(14.0)	(13.1)	(14.4)	(14.5)	(11.2)	(11.5)	(12.0)	(10.5)
R^2			0.856	0.873	0.841	0.875	0.877	0.842	0.850	0.845	0.825
Border effect		14.9	15.1	17.8	15.1	14.2	9.4	9.2	10.4	8.9

(Continued)

Table 2-3. (*continued*)

Coefficients (t-values)	1988	1989	1990	1991	1992	1993	1994	1995	1996
Saskatchewan: ln(DIST) = −2.494 (11.6)									
79 observations ln(GDP) = 1.102 (13.2)									
ln(REM) = −0.229 (1.9)									
OWN = −1.320 (1.3)									
Border coefficient	2.78	2.78	2.70	2.63	2.40	2.28	2.18	2.27	1.95
t-value	(9.5)	(9.4)	(9.4)	(9.0)	(8.6)	(8.2)	(7.5)	(7.8)	(6.6)
R^2		0.782	0.771	0.783	0.769	0.772	0.770	0.750	0.754	0.740
Border effect		16.1	16.1	14.9	13.8	11.0	9.7	8.8	9.6	7.0
Alberta: ln(DIST) = −1.926 (9.6)									
79 observations ln(GDP) = 1.020 (12.4)									
ln(REM) = −0.253 (2.5)									
OWN = −0.844 (−0.8)									
Border coefficient	2.25	2.12	2.11	2.04	1.92	1.99	2.02	1.95	1.75
t-value	(7.8)	(7.3)	(7.3)	(7.0)	(6.8)	(6.3)	(6.4)	(6.5)	(5.9)
R^2		0.759	0.735	0.754	0.731	0.730	0.675	0.661	0.677	0.680
Border effect		9.5	8.3	8.3	7.7	6.8	7.3	7.5	7.1	5.8
British Columbia: ln(DIST) = −1.085 (10.8)									
79 observations ln(GDP) = 0.935 (17.0)									
ln(REM) = −0.028 (0.5)									
OWN = 1.047 (1.6)									
Border coefficient	2.23	2.22	2.26	2.19	2.05	1.75	1.66	1.71	1.66
t-value	(10.3)	(11.5)	(10.7)	(10.7)	(10.8)	(8.6)	(8.3)	(8.7)	(9.0)
R^2		0.810	0.845	0.822	0.828	0.844	0.818	0.819	0.823	0.841
Border effect		9.3	9.2	9.6	8.9	7.8	5.8	5.3	5.5	5.2

indication that sales within provinces are higher than those among provinces, although the effect is statistically insignificant. The observations for internal sales are also included in the province-by-province equations, but the coefficients are in all cases insignificant.

One noteworthy feature of the province-by-province equations is that the remoteness variables are almost never significant. This implies that the significant effects of this variable in the full-sample equations are based on interprovincial differences in average remoteness. Also interesting are the differences from province to province in the effects of distance on trade. Distance effects are

substantially higher in Newfoundland and the three prairie provinces (Manitoba, Saskatchewan, and Alberta), and smaller in
Quebec, Ontario, and British Columbia, the three most populous
provinces. This may be a feature of industry mix, or perhaps of the
possibility that provinces containing the largest transportation
hubs offer better opportunities for low-cost transport to further
destinations.

All provinces show post-FTA reductions in border effects. Most
replicate the national pattern, including an absence of trend before
1990, a substantial reduction between 1990 and 1993, and rough
constancy from 1993 through 1996. The proportionate drops in
the border effect were largest in the western provinces, where
border effects were lower in the first place.

Moving from east to west, which is the order in which the results
are reported, the border effects are highest in two of the maritime
provinces (Nova Scotia and Prince Edward Island). They are
about the national average in Quebec, above the national average
in Ontario, and lowest in the three westernmost provinces. It
should be expected that border effects would be higher for
manufactured goods than for bulk resource commodities, and this
is confirmed by the results, as the ranking of border effects follows
the ranking in terms of resource dependence, with the lowest border
effects in the three western provinces with the largest concentrations
in the production and export of natural resource commodities.

If this is the correct interpretation of the small border effects in
Canada's three most western provinces, then we should expect to
find export border effects smaller than import ones for the
resource-dependent western provinces. To find separate export
and import border effects for each province, the HOME variable is
split into two variables, one relating to that province's interprovincial exports, and the other covering its imports.[24] Then a new
variable is introduced covering each province's exports to U.S.
states. All three dummy variables are included in the province-by-
province equations. The border coefficients reported in table 2-4
for imports are those on the interprovincial import variable. The
export coefficients shown in the table are calculated as the inter-

---

24. This is the same procedure used by Anderson and Smith (1997).

Table 2-4. *Border Coefficients by Direction of Trade*

	1988	1989	1990	1991	1992	1993	1994	1995	1996
Canada									
Imports	2.667	2.634	2.630	2.599	2.581	2.337	2.380	2.556	2.452
Exports	2.964	3.027	3.219	3.042	2.914	2.639	2.548	2.654	2.492
P-value of equality	.002	.000	.000	.000	.001	.002	.085	.323	.682
Newfoundland									
Imports	2.762	2.759	2.686	3.026	2.880	2.785	2.218	3.743	3.559
Exports	1.298	2.112	2.206	2.417	2.058	1.448	1.304	1.696	1.362
P-value of equality	.067	.509	.466	.452	.385	.150	.303	.041	.029
New Brunswick									
Imports	2.146	2.136	2.105	2.093	1.948	1.755	1.777	1.914	1.837
Exports	3.336	3.586	3.441	3.318	3.558	3.310	3.105	3.126	2.908
P-value of equality	.029	.013	.060	.048	.003	.005	.028	.035	.060
Nova Scotia									
Imports	3.301	3.246	3.105	3.051	3.137	3.007	3.305	3.349	3.473
Exports	3.365	3.341	3.848	3.187	2.958	2.807	2.756	2.938	2.972
P-value of equality	.917	.877	.144	.816	.774	.758	.333	.488	.386
Prince Edward Island									
Imports	2.625	2.447	2.816	2.436	2.643	2.490	2.959	3.082	2.826
Exports	3.059	2.845	3.490	3.512	3.663	3.094	2.989	3.101	2.856
P-value of equality	.586	.640	.401	.170	.139	.391	.969	.982	.968
Quebec									
Imports	2.449	2.406	2.505	2.379	2.329	2.022	2.113	2.265	2.215
Exports	3.157	3.149	3.385	3.165	2.916	2.620	2.440	2.444	2.315
P-value of equality	.028	.010	.003	.009	.032	.070	.298	.513	.726
Ontario									
Imports	2.679	2.762	2.648	2.612	2.522	2.337	2.190	2.092	2.187
Exports	3.626	3.629	3.882	3.745	3.436	3.202	3.049	2.984	2.935
P-value of equality	.006	.015	.001	.002	.010	.021	.019	.017	.040

Table 2-4. *(continued)*

	1988	1989	1990	1991	1992	1993	1994	1995	1996
Manitoba									
Imports	2.139	2.194	2.283	2.291	2.287	1.750	1.820	1.868	1.693
Exports	3.259	3.234	3.469	3.134	3.031	2.730	2.621	2.812	2.677
P-value of equality	.002	.002	.002	.011	.021	.006	.020	.006	.007
Saskatchewan									
Imports	2.427	2.389	2.420	2.348	2.204	2.025	2.036	1.861	1.522
Exports	3.154	3.195	2.999	2.919	2.597	2.533	2.321	2.669	2.369
P-value of equality	.155	.114	.253	.277	.432	.318	.595	.115	.106
Alberta									
Imports	2.049	2.011	1.864	1.926	1.857	1.670	1.716	1.781	1.672
Exports	2.431	2.211	2.331	2.132	1.961	2.276	2.276	2.096	1.795
P-value of equality	.466	.708	.373	.694	.836	.296	.326	.560	.813
British Columbia									
Imports	2.740	2.651	2.507	2.500	2.458	2.177	2.131	2.132	2.024
Exports	1.787	1.860	2.088	1.960	1.734	1.405	1.278	1.374	1.380
P-value of equality	.007	.015	.281	.143	.029	.029	.013	.029	.047

provincial export coefficient minus the U.S. export coefficient. The *P*-values shown below these coefficients are the Wald tests of equality between the import coefficient and the difference between the two export coefficients. When these *P*-values are low, then the difference between the import and export border effects is significant for that province in that year.

The results in table 2-4 do show that for Canada as a whole, the border effect at the start of the period was greater for southbound than for northbound trade, but has moved close to equality by the mid-1990s. It is important to note that table 2-4 shows border coefficients, and not the implied border effects, which are very much larger. British Columbia has the lowest export border coefficient, and for most years the export effect is significantly below the import effect for that province. The only other province where

the export effect is significantly below the import effect is Newfoundland. The pattern is not found in the other western provinces, where the low total effect comes more on the import side than
the export side. Most provinces mimic the national pattern, with
export border effects that have fallen more than import effects
during the post-FTA adjustment.

1990 Border Effects by Industry

Statistics Canada has recently prepared a disaggregated match-
ing of interprovincial and province-state trade for 1990. The previous section presented revised estimates of aggregate border
effects based on these new data. The disaggregated data for 1990
also permit exploration of the pattern of border effects on an
industry-by-industry basis. Knowledge of differences by industry
should make it easier to assess the various hypotheses about the
reasons for the very large border effects evident in the aggregate
data.

Data are available for twenty-seven goods-producing industries. In
order to make these data publishable, Statistics Canada has had to
censor observations where the number of market participants is so
small that knowing the total flow might permit inferences to be made
about the value of sales by individual firms. Greater disaggregation
means more lost observations, either because actual flows are zero, or
because flows have been censored to protect the confidentiality of the
data providers. The finer the detail, however, the more accurately can
interprovincial trade flows be matched with international flows. To
offer the best of both worlds, we consider results from five industry
groupings and then from the individual industries.

Table 2-5 shows the results of a five-way disaggregation of total
goods: transportation equipment (11 percent of the total, mainly
cars and parts); primary products (18 percent, mainly agricultural
products); natural resource products (22 percent, mainly lumber,
pulp and paper, metals, and energy); food and textiles (5 percent,
including tobacco and alcoholic beverages); and other manufactured products (39 percent). The remaining 5 percent represents
the observations that had to be excluded from the disaggregated

Table 2-5. *Border Effects by Major Industry, 1990*

	(i) Transportation	(ii) Primary products	(iii) Natural resource products	(iv) Food and textiles	(v) Other manufactured products	(vi) Total	(vii) Transportation
Observations	546	630	620	551	659	680	546
Constant	−12.1	−0.44	−7.49	−8.36	−7.28	−4.11	−11.6
	(8.8)	(0.4)	(6.8)	(6.9)	(8.6)	(5.6)	(8.5)
ln(GDPx)	1.64	0.817	1.21	1.36	1.61	1.27	1.61
	(23.9)	(15.8)	(23.3)	(22.7)	(42.6)	(40.0)	(23.6)
ln(GDPm)	0.934	1.07	1.19	0.671	0.765	0.954	0.901
	(15.9)	(19.4)	(24.8)	(13.1)	(21.5)	(30.5)	(15.5)
ln(DIST)	−1.28	−1.88	−1.56	−1.12	−1.44	−1.46	−1.26
	(10.0)	(16.3)	(15.0)	(10.1)	(17.7)	(20.3)	(9.9)
ln(REMx)	−0.688	1.46	0.934	−0.523	0.311	0.656	−0.650
	(3.5)	(8.0)	(5.7)	(3.0)	(2.4)	(5.8)	(3.3)
ln(REMm)	0.581	0.071	0.101	0.620	0.728	0.284	0.627
	(2.9)	(0.4)	(0.6)	(3.6)	(5.7)	(2.5)	(3.2)
HOME	3.38	3.99	2.57	3.66	2.40	3.02	3.39
	(12.6)	(18.6)	(13.0)	(17.5)	(15.9)	(22.8)	(12.9)
CAR	...	...	...	...	...	...	3.19
							(3.5)
PLANE	...	...	...	...	...	...	2.60
							(2.9)
$\bar{R}^2$	0.617	0.597	0.653	0.606	0.777	0.797	0.629
SEE	1.81	1.76	1.57	1.58	1.26	1.12	1.78
Border effect	29.2	53.9	13.1	38.7	11.0	20.5	29.5
Border effect for car producers							1.2
Border effect for plane producers							2.2

Notes: Absolute values of *t*-statistics are in parentheses. The dependent variable is the natural log of total shipments of goods from province or state *x* to province or state *m*, with ln(GDPx) being the log of the exporter's GDP and ln(GDPm) of the importer's GDP. HOME takes the value 1.0 for each observation recording trade from one province to another.

series to protect confidentiality. What might we expect to find when comparing the results across industries? We would expect to find border effects larger where there are larger formal barriers to trade, smaller distance effects for products with high value-to-weight ratios, and perhaps smaller border effects for products in which comparative advantage differs greatly on the two sides of the border.

What do the results show? Border effects are large in all industries, being lower than average in the "resource" and "other manufacturing" sectors. For the resource products sector, the low border effect may be attributable to the importance of comparative advantage trade, although the border effect even here is still strikingly large. The distance effect is lowest in the food and textiles industry, where the value-to-weight ratio is high. The border effect is also highest in that industry (as can be seen from the more disaggregated results in table 2.6, where the high border effect for primary products is derived entirely from its food components), for which the border still represents the locus of tariff and nontariff limitations on trade. Taste differences in this industry may also segment national markets from one another. The other manufacturing sector, which covers a wide variety of products, including machinery and equipment, has the lowest border effect and the best fit of all the equations, as might be expected of the largest and most diversified category.

The biggest puzzle, at least at first glance, is posed by the results for transportation equipment, comprising mainly cars, trucks, and parts, but also including planes and aircraft parts. Our results replicate the finding of Anderson and Smith that the border effect is significantly higher for transportation equipment than for other industries.[25] This result is so puzzling to them and others because the 1965 Auto Pact between Canada and the United States permitted auto producers to move cars and parts freely between the two countries with no tariffs or other border costs. Since the North American car industry was then dominated by the big three manufacturers, who already had major plants on both sides of the border, it was to be expected that the Auto Pact would be followed by a large-scale rationalization of production. A substantial increase in bilateral trade was expected as one of the consequences of this rationalization.

This is just what happened. In 1964 cars and parts comprised only 2 percent of total merchandise exports and 11 percent of imports. Adjustment to the new arrangements was rapid, so that by 1968 trade in cars and parts had risen to 20 percent of exports and 25 percent of imports, well above their current shares.[26] It was the perceived success

25. See Anderson and Smith (1996).

26. Statistics Canada, Dominion Bureau of Statistics, External Trade Division, *Trade of Canada: Imports by Countries,* January-December 1964, table 2; Bank of Canada (1969), merchandise import tables.

of the Auto Pact in rationalizing production and increasing trade, while achieving and then maintaining fairly balanced total production on the two sides of the border, that led the Canadian government, following the advice of the Royal Commission on the Economic Union and Development Prospects for Canada (1984), to propose the Canada–U.S. FTA, the precursor to NAFTA, to an initially skeptical U.S. administration in 1984. Thus it comes as a surprise to find a 1990 border effect for transportation equipment of 29, almost 50 percent more than the average for all goods, twenty-five years after the Auto Pact came into effect.

Perhaps the key to the puzzle, as suggested earlier in the chapter, is the fact that the Auto Pact applied to transactions by car producers, and not by consumers, distributors, and retailers. Thus it is possible that the border effect is low between states and provinces that are homes to the auto industry, and high for all other trading pairs. This proposition is easy to test, since the auto industry has a very high geographic concentration in both countries. In the United States, Michigan's share of total nonfarm labor force in the automobile industry is much higher than that of any other state. Ohio is also important in the U.S. car industry, although much less so than Michigan. Washington and California, especially the former, are important in the aircraft industry. In Canada, Ontario and Quebec are the key players in both industries.

Testing the hypothesis requires the construction of a special variable, called "CAR" in table 2-5, that takes the value of 1.0 for each international trade flow relating to shipments from one major car-producing state or province to another. Its four observations cover shipments in both directions between Michigan and Ontario and between Michigan and Quebec. A parallel variable called "PLANE" covers shipments in both directions between Washington state, and Ontario and Quebec. Both variables are highly significant in equation (vii) of table 2-5. Tests show that including a larger group of less important producing states and provinces gives less precise results than the simpler version shown here.[27]

---

27. In particular, an additional variable covering shipments between Ohio and both Ontario and Quebec had the expected positive sign, but the coefficient was small and insignificant. A similar variable for California took a coefficient of about half the size of that

Interpretation of the results is quite straightforward, and entirely in accord with the hypothesis. The net border effect for trade in transportation equipment between the major producing units on either side of the border is obtained as the antilog of the difference between the main border effect and the coefficient on either CAR or PLANE. As can be seen from the calculations at the bottom of table 2-5, the net border effect for trade between the car-producing states and provinces is 1.2, insignificantly different from the 1.0 value that represents no border effect at all. Thus the trade-creating effects of the Auto Pact, combined with the unified ownership and operation of the major North American car producers, have eliminated the border effect at the producer level, but only for transborder shipments of cars and parts to and from Michigan, Ontario, and Quebec. For the rest of both countries, sales across provincial borders remain almost thirty times as likely as sales across the national border, after adjusting for the effects of economic size and distance. It remains to be seen whether this very high border effect at the wholesale, retail, and consumer levels will survive intact following the gradual post-FTA elimination of the previous barriers to transborder shipments by distributors and consumers.

The effect of the PLANE variable is significant, but the interpretation here is somewhat different. As expected, the aircraft industry effect is smaller than that for cars,[28] since there was no aircraft industry analogue to the 1965 Auto Pact. High levels of transportation equipment trade between Washington state and

---

for Washington and had a t-value of 1.6. Although California and Washington state each have about 18 percent of national employment in the production of aircraft and parts (Bureau of Labor Statistics, 1996, *State and Area Employment, Hours, and Earnings; Aircraft and Parts Industry*), this amounts to almost ten times more specialization in Washington than in California, given the relative size of the two states. Quebec and Ontario have 50 percent and 38 percent (Statistics Canada, 1982, *General Review of Manufacturing Industries of Canada; Transportation Equipment Industries, Aircraft and Aircraft Parts Manufacturers*), respectively, of national employment in aircraft and parts, so there are no other contenders for inclusion in Canada. Since moving further down the list of producing states provides no further information, beyond further support for the notion that bilateral trade flows are more intense between the largest producers, the use of Michigan and Washington as the states specialized in autos and aircraft, respectively, appears to be justified.

28. The difference between the two effects is not statistically significant, and the two can be restricted to be equal with no loss of adjusted goodness of fit.

both Ontario and Quebec probably reflected initially some production-sharing arrangements pursuant to Canadian purchases of military and civilian aircraft. Subsequently, the pattern was probably maintained through common ownership and later sharing of markets and production based on specialization by size of aircraft.

It is notable that allowing for the specially tight linkages between the car- and plane-producing states and provinces has no effect at all on the estimate of the general border effect, even for the transportation equipment industry itself. This is a consequence of the geographic concentration of the auto and aircraft industries, since only slightly more than 1 percent of the observations are transborder shipments between producing states and provinces.

If this unravelling of the transportation industry puzzle is convincing, there do not seem to remain any major surprises or puzzles in table 2-5. Most of the interindustry differences in coefficients are not significant, and the patterns that do exist appear broadly consistent with differences in their products and structures. Thus the major industry results tend to confirm their aggregate counterparts by providing some assurance that the aggregate border effects have their appropriate counterparts in the component industries.

To provide a further level of confirmation, table 2-6 contains comparable results for twenty-six component industries, classified according to the major industry group to which they were assigned for the equations reported in table 2-5. The transportation equipment industry does not reappear in table 2-6, since it had a category of its own in table 2-5. Within the primary category, the border effects are largest for those industries with domestic supply management arrangements. These are most clearly exemplified by agriculture, with border effects of almost 100 in meat, fish, and dairy; over 80 in fruit, vegetables, and feed; 65 for grains; and 30 for other agricultural commodities. Only for metallic ores and concentrates, a small category, are the border effects very small (3); for most of the other categories they are about 50 percent higher than for merchandise trade in total.

Among the resource-based manufacturing products, there appears to have been an aggregation bias at work in the table 2-5 equation, as

Table 2-6. *Border Effects for Twenty-Six Industries, 1990*

Industry group	Observations	Percent of total trade	t-statistic on border coefficient	$\bar{R}^2$	SEE	Border effect
Primary						
Grains	218	0.54	10.02	0.35	2.06	64.84
Other agricultural	516	3.57	12.02	0.52	1.74	30.53
Forestry	161	0.14	6.39	0.37	1.90	28.19
Fishing and trapping	134	0.64	4.99	0.30	1.94	12.08
Metallic ores and concentrates	142	0.85	1.17	0.25	2.56	3.04
Mineral fuels	108	2.73	3.77	0.30	3.17	30.44
Meat, fish, and dairy	488	5.30	18.42	0.54	1.79	98.98
Fruit, vegetables, feed, miscellaneous food	483	3.45	17.49	0.54	1.75	82.92
Resource						
Lumber, sawmill, other wood	518	4.92	12.59	0.47	1.86	27.66
Paper and paper products	533	8.89	10.91	0.55	1.80	23.65
Primary metals	489	3.61	13.88	0.66	1.60	36.40
Nonmetallic minerals	383	1.32	7.21	0.33	3.61	23.35
Petroleum and coal	351	3.10	6.84	0.34	2.41	45.07
Food and textiles						
Beverages	268	0.54	11.12	0.42	1.82	45.91
Tobacco and tobacco products	81	0.13	2.70	0.12	2.10	71.57
Textiles and textile products	451	1.77	12.94	0.56	1.67	30.87
Knitted products and clothing	448	2.18	16.46	0.50	1.67	85.79
Manufacturing						
Rubber, leather, and plastic	508	3.09	13.70	0.68	1.38	27.64
Furniture and fixtures	437	0.86	15.91	0.61	1.56	55.39
Printing and publishing	529	1.78	17.24	0.61	1.63	47.21
Metal	551	3.09	20.16	0.72	1.38	38.51
Machinery and equipment	612	10.93	10.45	0.69	1.42	7.14
Electrical and communications	533	6.88	13.48	0.66	1.62	27.27
Nonmetallic mineral products	447	1.19	15.07	0.63	1.52	38.65
Chemicals	547	7.64	11.43	0.57	1.77	17.21
Miscellaneous manufacturing	572	5.05	11.00	0.67	1.46	9.11

each of the component industries has an estimated border effect higher than that which appeared in the total equation. Exact comparisons are made difficult by the fact that the number of observations is different in each of the industries, reflecting the differing patterns and volumes of trade in the various products. In the food and textile group, the border effects are largest in tobacco and knitwear, while above the national averages in all cases.

Only in the manufacturing sector are there any large industries with border effects well below the national average. These are machinery and equipment (11 percent of total trade, with a border effect of 7), and miscellaneous manufacturing (5 percent of total trade, with a border effect of 9). Canada has traditionally had a very high import share in machinery and equipment investment spending, perhaps due in part to the high foreign-ownership share in manufacturing. The low border effect in this industry is thus due to high northbound rather than southbound flows. For most of the other manufacturing sectors, the border effects are well above the national average, rising to almost 50 for printing and publishing and to 55 for furniture and fixtures.

Looking over the results of all twenty-seven industries, comprising the transportation equipment industry from table 2-5 and the twenty-six industries in table 2-6, twenty of the twenty-seven have estimated border effects greater than 25, and in nine of these cases the effect exceeds 40. Only in four of the industries was the estimated effect less than 15. Thus the industry detail suggests that border effects are large and pervasive throughout the range of industries engaged in interprovincial and international trade.

Trade in Services

However difficult the data situation is for merchandise trade, it is worse for services. National economies have become much more service oriented during the second half of the twentieth century, while international trade has traditionally been much lower in services than in merchandise. At the same time, international trade in services, while starting from a much smaller base, has grown much faster than international merchandise trade. Comparing

Table 2-7. *Border Effects for Services, 1988–96*

Year	(i) *Interprovincial/* *international* *for services*	(ii) *Interprovincial/* *international* *for goods*	(iii) *Services/goods*	(iv) *Border effect for* *services*
1988	1.576	0.720	2.188	37.0
1989	1.574	0.735	2.139	36.0
1990	1.532	0.702	2.183	42.6
1991	1.458	0.642	2.269	38.7
1992	1.400	0.569	2.460	37.5
1993	1.329	0.508	2.613	32.0
1994	1.205	0.466	2.584	29.5
1995	1.189	0.433	2.746	38.5
1996	1.168	0.434	2.690	32.1

goods and services, current international trade densities are much less for services, on average, than for goods. Since domestic final demand for services is also growing faster than for goods, it is not immediately clear whether the two markets are approaching the same degree of relative internationalization. A working hypothesis might be that some services may now be more tradable than goods, and others less, with the relationship between the aggregates possibly differing from country to country. As chapter 4 discusses, financial services are among the most internationally mobile, and represent a special case needing special treatment.

There are no measures of bilateral trade in services among provinces in Canada, and no measures of service trade between individual provinces and U.S. states. Thus we cannot repeat for services the analysis just completed for merchandise trade. However, the Canadian provincial accounts do contain data on a province-by-province basis separately for goods and service exports, so it is possible to compare the ratios of foreign to domestic sales for goods and services. As might be expected, international exports and imports, relative to either total production or domestic consumption, are much higher for goods than for services. Simple comparison of the two ratios suggests that border effects are more than twice as large for services as they are for goods, as shown in column (iv) of table 2-7. To compute the ratios in the first columns, we first calculate separately for services (nonmerchandise) trade and for merchandise trade the ratio of interprovincial to international shipments. The results show that both markets were becoming less focused on domestic sales over the nine-year period, with the trend more marked for goods than for services. Column (iii) shows the relative domestic focus of service trade compared to goods, calculated as the ratio of column (i) to column (ii). These figures measure the domestic orientation of service trade compared to that for goods, on the implicit assumption that the same foreign market sizes and distances are relevant for both.

Column (iii) shows that markets for services are between two and three times more focused on domestic customers than are those for goods, with some evidence of a rising trend in the last ten years. How can this be reconciled with other evidence that global trade in services has been rising faster than that for merchandise? There are two parts to the explanation. On the one hand, service industries have in total been growing substantially faster than goods industries, and, more important, in the early years of the 1990s Canada's merchandise trade linkages with the United States were being tightened as a consequence of the U.S.–Canada FTA. As a result, Canada's merchandise trade grew faster than service trade over this period, in contrast to general global trends.

To get a rough measure of the border effect for services, we can then multiply the figures in column (iii) by the estimated border effects for merchandise trade obtained from table 2-1, column (v), for 1990, from table 2-2 for 1991 through 1996, and from analogous equations estimated for 1988 and 1989. The results are shown in column (iv). Border effects for services appear to range from about 30 to just above 42, with some evidence of a downward trend since 1990. The post-FTA value, as of 1996, appears to be about 32.

A more direct estimate of border effects for one important service is available from an early application of the gravity model to a sample of within-province, interprovincial, and U.S.-bound long-distance telephone calls originating in Montreal in 1954. A simple version of the gravity model revealed a border effect of 50 between Quebec and the United States, five to ten times larger than the corresponding border effects between Ontario and

Quebec.[29] Language differences are no doubt partially responsible for both boundary effects, while the much higher effects at the national border are probably traceable to the differences in the densities of cultural, commercial, institutional, and migration linkages studied in this and subsequent chapters. The magnitude of the border effect for telephone calls in 1954 is even higher than that for total services in the late 1980s. The two estimates are close enough, and the data sources different enough, to make the two results mutually supportive, with a hint, needing testing, that border effects for telephone calls may well have fallen in the second half of the century.

29. See Mackay (1958). The results from Montreal data were also confirmed with data for calls originating in Quebec, Sherbrooke, Toronto, Vancouver, and Winnipeg, with the densities found for calls among English-speaking cities to be similar to those among French-speaking cities.

Chapter 3

International Merchandise Trade

TWO PRINCIPAL difficulties must be faced in applying the gravity model to estimate border effects using international data. First, there are relatively few countries with comparable data for both production and exports of merchandise; second, there are generally no data for the distance of shipment for domestic sales. The former difficulty restricts the sample to countries with reasonably complete sets of input-output data, since these typically involve reconciliations and divisions of gross shipments of goods, usually disaggregated by industry, between domestic and foreign markets. This chapter initially makes use of international trade flows among twenty-two Organization for Economic Cooperation and Development (OECD) countries, and later adds eleven developing countries. Estimates of border effects will be based only on countries for which there are direct measures of domestic sales. These include sixteen of the original OECD members plus all of the eleven additional countries. The sample period generally runs from 1988 through 1992, although for several of the newly added countries domestic sales data are available for only some of the years, requiring the sample to be adjusted accordingly.

The second problem is that there are no data available for domestic trade distances. We generally follow the procedure suggested by Wei (1996), where domestic sales distances are approximated, in the absence of more specific information, as one-quarter of the distance between a country and its nearest trading partner. For Canada, where input-output tables are available by province, and where data are also available for interprovincial shipments, it is possible to calculate an average internal trade distance based on a weighted average of the interprovincial trade distances and some assumed distances for intraprovincial shipments. As it happens, this produces an internal trade distance that is very close to that obtained from the Wei assumption, but there is no assurance that this comforting similarity can be carried over to countries with very different geographic and economic structures. Thus it will be necessary to run sensitivity tests based on alternative means of estimating internal trade distances to ensure that any conclusions do not depend overmuch on the essentially unmeasured internal trade distances. This hole in the available data for the gravity model perhaps helps to explain why there have not been earlier attempts to measure the relative intensities of internal and external trade linkages, and may eventually force greater reliance on the results based on the more comparably measured Canadian data for interprovincial and province-state trade flows and distances.

A word of explanation is in order about the distinction made here between the OECD and developing countries. OECD membership is growing, and at any time both OECD and non-OECD countries differ greatly amongst themselves in their levels and patterns of economic development. Thus too much significance should not be attached to whether a particular country is considered part of the OECD group, which comprises the largest number of OECD countries for which appropriate data were available when the first estimation attempts were made. The additional eleven countries comprise all those for which data are available for both domestic and international shipments of goods, as signaled by a sufficiently complete table 4-1 in the *United Nations National Accounts Statistics*. Although average per capita incomes in the original group of twenty-two countries are several times higher than those in the eleven additional countries, there is enough heterogeneity among the two groups to provide some overlap. For example, Mexico, which joined the OECD in 1994 and thus became one of the original twenty-two countries, had a 1992 per capita income just over half that of Korea, which joined the OECD in late 1996 and is thus one of the eleven additional countries. Although the ranges of incomes, policies, and trade patterns differ so much among countries as to make it somewhat arbitrary to divide them into two groups even casually labeled as "OECD" and "developing countries," the same variety is good for estimation. The two subsamples, and especially the total sample, provide enough range of experience to identify relationships that do or do not apply equally well to countries in very different circumstances. Fortunately, any ambiguities about the split between OECD and non-OECD countries will not affect the interpretation of the final results, since we find that the inclusion of a variable that makes the size of the border effect smaller as per capita incomes rise allows the OECD and non-OECD countries to be easily included in the same sample.

Results Using Data for Merchandise Trade among OECD Countries

Our data for OECD countries include bilateral trade among twenty-two countries and own-shipments estimates for sixteen countries, for each year from 1988 through 1992. Table 3-1 shows the 1992 results for several different specifications of the gravity model, while table 3-2 shows the results of the preferred specification for each of the years 1988 to 1992. The first equation in Table 3-1 shows the basic bilateral gravity equation, with the implied border effects reported at the bottom of the table. The base assumption about internal trade distances is that they are one-quarter of the distance between a country and its nearest trading partner. Distances between nations are approximated by the distances between their capital cities, following the assumption made previously in Wei (1996) and Helliwell (1997). Since the information content of these assumptions is low, tests were run involving doubling and halving the assumed distances. As shown in equation (i), the border effect from the basic gravity model is about 10. Halving the internal distances (as in equation [ii]) reduces the border effect to 5.4, while doubling the distances (as in equation

Table 3-1. *OECD Merchandise Trade, 1992*

	Equation						
	(i)	*(ii)*	*(iii)*	*(iv)*	*(v)*	*(vi)*	*(vii)*
Constant	4.83	4.83	4.83	0.39	1.11	1.41	2.06
	(15.8)	(15.8)	(15.8)	(0.4)	(1.3)	(1.6)	(2.5)
ln(GDPx)	0.771	0.771	0.771	0.731	0.728	0.733	1.28
	(31.8)	(31.8)	(31.8)	(29.6)	(30.2)	(30.5)	(16.4)
ln(GDPm)	0.773	0.772	0.773	0.733	0.730	0.735	0.800
	(32.3)	(32.3)	(32.3)	(30.0)	(30.6)	(30.9)	(10.5)
ln(DIST)	−0.865	−0.865	−0.865	−1.02	−0.941	−0.937	−0.890
	(28.4)	(28.3)	(28.4)	(24.8)	(20.5)	(20.5)	(20.2)
EU members	...	...	...	...	0.239	0.230	0.420
					(2.3)	(2.2)	(4.1)
Common language	...	...	...	...	0.568	0.574	0.565
					(5.2)	(5.3)	(5.5)
ln(REMx)	...	...	...	0.338	0.235	0.208	0.438
				(3.6)	(2.5)	(2.2)	(4.6)
ln(REMm)	...	...	...	0.532	0.430	0.404	0.464
				(5.6)	(4.6)	(4.3)	(4.9)
HOME	2.29	1.69	3.24	1.73	2.12	2.12	2.29
	(10.4)	(7.3)	(15.6)	(7.3)	(8.5)	(8.5)	(9.6)
HOME × ln($Y/\overline{Y}$)	...	...	...	...	...	−0.820	−1.31
						(2.4)	(3.9)
ln(POPx)	...	...	...	...	...	...	−0.600
							(7.3)
ln(POPm)	...	...	...	...	...	...	−0.086
							(1.1)
$\overline{R}^2$	0.874	0.874	0.874	0.882	0.889	0.890	0.901
SEE	0.775	0.775	0.775	0.751	0.729	0.725	0.688
Border effects							
OECD average	9.8	5.4	25.5	5.7			
OECD unrelated	...	...	...	...	8.3	8.3	9.9
EU-EU trade	...	...	...	...	6.5	6.6	6.5
Common language	...	...	...	...	4.7	4.7	5.6
EU-EU plus common language	...	...	...	...	3.7	3.7	3.7

Sources: Sources for tables 3-1–3-5 are author's calculations using the following sources:
OECD and non-OECD trade flows are taken from International Monetary Fund. 1995. *Direction of Trade Statistics Yearbook.* Washington.
OECD GDP/per capita income, non-OECD per capita income, and all population figures are from World Bank. 1994. *World Tables: 1994.* Johns Hopkins University Press.
Non-OECD GDP figures are from table 1.1 and non-OECD merchandise sales are from table 4.1 in United Nations. 1996. *National Accounts Statistics: Main Aggregates and Detailed Tables, 1993.* New York.
Notes: Estimated by OLS with 465 observations, dependent variable ln(Sxm). Absolute values of t-statistics are shown in parentheses below the coefficients.

[iii]) raises the border effect to 25.5.[1] The appropriate conclusion is that the estimates of border effects are sufficiently dependent on the data for average internal trade distances to encourage more detailed investigation of the geography of internal trade, to either support or replace the assumptions currently being used for internal trade distances. This is of greatest importance when attention is on the relative values of border effects among countries. For the average results, there are no feasible values for internal trade distance low enough to make the border effect disappear.

Equation (iv) extends the basic gravity model by adding remoteness measures for both exporting and importing countries. Comparing equations (i) and (iv) shows that adding the remoteness variables cuts the border effect by almost half, to 5.7. This is a much larger impact than in the case of province-state trade, perhaps reflecting greater variability of remoteness among OECD countries than among provinces and states. However, in the global sample, where distances vary still more, the remoteness variables are insignificant and have no effect on the value of the border coefficient.

Equation (v) adds variables for common language and membership in the European Union (EU). The language variable takes the value of 1.0 for each international trade flow from one country to another sharing a common official language. Thus it takes the value of 1.0 for trade between Switzerland and each of France, Germany, and Italy, since French, German, and Italian are all official languages in Switzerland. The language variable is expected to take a positive coefficient, by reducing the costs and increasing the extent of transborder contacts and information flows. Since language is not independent of culture, nations that share a common language also often share to some extent common history, institutions, and values. Platteau (1994) argues that shared values and institutions are likely to reduce the costs of making and enforcing contracts, since shared values reduce the extent of uncertainties that otherwise might require negotiation and fine print

---

1. The same is true in the global sample, where halving the internal trade distances also halves the border effect, and doubling the distances doubles the border effect. This follows directly from a gravity model with a distance elasticity near unity.

to sort out, or costly legal actions to resolve. All of the reasons that support the likely importance of a common language as a determinant of the tightness of trading links also support the existence of border effects more generally, since national borders, like languages, often serve to delineate populations with shared institutions and values. A common language has a large and significant effect on trade intensity. Two countries sharing a language are estimated to have two-way trade flows more than 50 percent larger than those between two otherwise similar countries.

The EU variable takes the value of 1.0 for each trade flow from one EU member to another. It is expected to take a positive coefficient to reflect the lower trade barriers and more harmonized regulations among EU countries than between them and their other trading partners. This effect is found in the data, although its size and significance are about half as great as for those sharing a common language. Thus trade among EU members is estimated to be about one-quarter greater than that between otherwise similar pairs of countries not sharing EU membership.[2]

Interpretation of national border effects becomes more complicated with the addition of other variables affecting the international flows of goods among subsets of countries. The border effect measures how much greater are domestic sales than those between the domestic economy and other countries, after allowing for the effects of economic size, distance, and alternative trading opportunities. Before these additional variables are added, the border effects reflect average values for all countries in the sample. After qualitative variables relating to some bilateral trade flows have been added, the border effects for a given country depend on which trading partners are being considered. For trade between one OECD country and another, where the two countries share

2. Many previous studies have estimated the effects of trading blocs on the strength of trade linkages, although not in a way that permits comparison of trade densities within trade blocs to those within nations. For example, Aitken (1973) and De Grauwe (1988) analyzed the effects of the European Economic Community and European Free Trade Association (EFTA) on European trading patterns; Bayoumi and Eichengreen (1995) used a gravity model to estimate trade diversion and trade creation effects of the European Community and EFTA; and Frankel and Wei (1993, 1994) and Frankel, Stein, and Wei (1995) have fitted gravity models to bilateral trade data to estimate the trade effects of several trade blocs and regional groupings.

neither a common language nor membership in the EU, the border effect is simply the antilog of the border variable (HOME) coefficient, shown in table 3-1 as the border effect for trade between unrelated OECD countries. These trading pairs represent 70 percent of the 465 observations in the sample.[3] To find the extent to which an EU member has domestic trade intensity greater than that with a fellow EU member, the border effect is equal to the antilog of the amount by which the HOME coefficient exceeds the EU coefficient.[4] The results show that border effects are very large even among the EU countries, with domestic trade intensities being six times greater than those between two EU countries.[5] A similar calculation shows the effects of sharing a common language, or of sharing both EU membership and a common language, as shown at the bottom of table 3-1.

Per Capita Incomes and Border Effects

Equation (vi) of table 3-1 includes a variable designed to test the extent to which the border effect differs according to the level of a country's per capita income. There is theory and empirical evidence to support this extension of the gravity model. Wei showed country-by-country estimates of border effects for OECD countries, and the richer countries tended to have smaller border effects.[6] Why is this likely to be the case? There are several reasons, which are not mutually exclusive. Each relates to a different conception of how and why international trade takes place. If trade is

3. Of the 465 observations, 12 percent relate to trade between countries sharing a common language, 20 percent cover trade from one EU country to another, and 1.3 percent relate to trade between two countries sharing both EU membership and a common language.

4. Taking the example of equation (v) of table 3-1, the border effect comparing domestic trade to that with fellow EU members is thus $\exp(2.12 - 0.239) = 6.6$. To find the extent to which domestic trade intensity is greater than that between one EU country and another sharing a common language, the border effect is calculated as $\exp(2.12 - 0.239 - 0.568) = 3.7$.

5. This sixfold border effect for trade among the EU counties mirrors exactly the earlier results obtained by Bröcker (1984), who fitted a gravity model, including a border variable, to 1970 road tonnage data for bilateral shipments among fifty-seven European regions.

6. See Wei (1996). This pattern was confirmed by subsequent regression analysis in Helliwell (1997).

based on a desire for a greater variety of differentiated products, each of which has some fixed costs of production or some other source of increasing returns to scale, then anything that increases the demand for product variety will increase the density of international trade. It is fairly plausible to suppose that increases in average per capita incomes will be accompanied by increasing knowledge of, and demand for, a greater variety of goods and services. The combination of increasing demand for product variety and increasing returns to scale in the production of specific goods would give rise to deeper trade networks as income increases.

However, all that theory demands is that consumers be willing to go farther afield for new products. Naturally, since average trading distances are greater for foreign trade than for domestic trade, this suggests an increase in the simple ratio of foreign to domestic trade as incomes increase. In the context of a gravity model including distance as a separate variable, the result of the increased demand for variety as incomes increase should be reflected in a smaller negative effect of distance on the trade of the higher-income countries, whose residents are willing to pay higher transport costs in order to get the product variety they crave. Thus this theory does not require or imply a drop in the relative demand for home goods, as opposed to goods produced closer to home, unless there are independent reasons to suppose that national boundaries affect tastes, technologies, institutions, or trading costs. If significant national differences exist in any of these factors, in addition to distance-related differences, then income-induced increases in the demand for product variety are likely to be associated with declines in the relative demand for home-produced goods, and hence with a decline in the border effect. Thus the finding of a border effect that declines as average incomes rise can be treated as support for the joint hypothesis that the demand for product variety increases with income and that there are substantial national border effects arising from differences in tastes, technologies, or institutions.

Other theories of trade might also be consistent with the finding of national border effects dropping as average incomes rise, although all seem to require the preexistence of border effects beyond the effects of distance. Some theories, however, would not imply any income effect on the size of the border coefficient. A model of comparative advantage trade limited by trade barriers would not seem to predict any influence of average incomes on the size of border effects. Thus if further research supports the income responsiveness of border effects, it should help to influence the balance of evidence about the relevance of different trade theories in predicting the volumes of domestic and international trade.

What is the current state of the evidence about the importance of income levels as determinants of border effects? The OECD results, as shown in equation (vi) of table 3-1, imply an elasticity of the border effect of −0.82 in response to increases in average per capita incomes. Per capita income is measured relative to the geometric average per capita income in the same year in all of the other countries in the sample, in this case twenty-two OECD countries.[7] The variable in the equation is equal to relative per capita income multiplied by the HOME variable, so that the coefficient on the HOME variable measures the border effect for a country with OECD-average per capita incomes. Further evidence on the role of per capita income as a determinant of relative border effects are reported in the next section, where it will be seen that border effects are far higher for the developing countries than for the OECD countries, but that relative incomes are sufficient to explain these differences.

Population, Per Capita Incomes, and Trade Flows

Many gravity models include population and per capita incomes as separate determinants of trade flows, under the supposition that the pure effects of scale, as represented by population, are

7. For each country the variable thus has a single observation, appearing in the row showing domestic sales, equal to the log of income per capita minus the mean of the logarithms of per capita income in twenty-two OECD countries. This permits the coefficient on the HOME variable to show the border effect for a country with average income equal to the OECD average, with border effects for specific countries measured as $\exp(h - b \times \text{coypc})$, where h is the coefficient on HOME, b is the coefficient on the relative income variable coypc, and coypc is the log difference between a country's per capita income and the OECD average for the year in question.

likely to be less than those of income per capita. This is consistent with trade models where the demand for tradable goods, and for increasing variety, grows faster than per capita incomes.[8] The trade data for provinces and states do not show systematic differences between the effects of population growth and those of per capita income growth, possibly because the variation of both incomes and tastes is less among states and provinces than among countries. Equation (vii) tests the hypothesis for the OECD sample and shows fairly strong evidence, at least for 1992, that the elasticities of trade with respect to per capita incomes are higher than those with respect to population, but significantly so only for exporters. This is revealed by the significant negative effect of the logarithm of exporter population in an equation already including the logarithm of aggregate gross domestic product (GDP). The net elasticity with respect to income per capita is thus equal to that for GDP, while that for population is equal to the net of the GDP and population coefficients. The former is significantly above 1.0, while the latter is approximately equal to unity, at least in the 1992 equation.

To show the extent to which these effects and others are replicated across years, table 3-2 shows the same equation estimated separately for each year from 1988 through 1992. The sample of 465 observations, the same as that used in table 3-1, is less than 484 because it excludes all observations having zero values for the dependent variable in any of the five years. Sample size is thus the same in each year, and any parameter trends can be taken to reflect changes in behavior or institutions rather than changes in the selection of countries. Separate estimation is undertaken for each year because Wald tests reject the imposition of common values for several of the key coefficients, especially those relating to GDP and population. Coefficients on exporter GDP show a steady upward trend while those on exporter population become steadily more

8. In Bergstrand (1989), the assumption of tastes for imported goods (presumed to be luxuries) rising with per capita incomes was used to support the presumption and finding of a positive effect of per capita incomes in the importing country. To explain the positive finding for exporter per capita income, he assumed that per capita income was a proxy for capital intensity, with a positive coefficient suggesting that the class of goods was relatively capital intensive.

Table 3-2. *OECD Merchandise Trade, 1988–92*

	1988	1989	1990	1991	1992
Constant	3.17	3.48	2.68	2.58	2.07
	(3.8)	(4.5)	(3.4)	(3.1)	(2.5)
ln(GDPx)	1.08	1.11	1.13	1.21	1.28
	(16.8)	(16.6)	(16.0)	(16.2)	(16.4)
ln(GDPm)	0.828	0.832	0.791	0.823	0.800
	(13.2)	(12.7)	(11.4)	(11.3)	(10.5)
ln(DIST)	−0.910	−0.904	−0.888	−0.900	−0.890
	(19.0)	(19.5)	(19.3)	(20.0)	(20.2)
EU members	0.419	0.462	0.418	0.451	0.420
	(3.8)	(4.2)	(3.9)	(4.3)	(4.1)
Common language	0.587	0.570	0.571	0.528	0.565
	(5.3)	(5.3)	(5.3)	(5.0)	(5.5)
ln(REMx)	0.283	0.235	0.263	0.373	0.438
	(3.1)	(2.8)	(2.9)	(4.0)	(4.6)
ln(REMm)	0.330	0.355	0.391	0.397	0.464
	(3.7)	(4.2)	(4.4)	(4.3)	(4.9)
HOME	2.35	2.31	2.33	2.27	2.29
	(8.5)	(9.3)	(9.4)	(9.3)	(9.6)
HOME × ln($Y/\overline{Y}$)					
ln(POPx)	−0.359	−0.400	−0.411	−0.508	−0.599
	(5.4)	(5.7)	(5.6)	(6.5)	(7.3)
ln(POPm)	−0.087	−0.088	−0.051	−0.091	−0.080
	(1.3)	(1.3)	(0.7)	(1.2)	(1.1)
$\overline{R}^2$	0.889	0.894	0.895	0.899	0.901
SEE	0.733	0.716	0.711	0.700	0.688
Border effects					
OECD unrelated	10.5	10.1	10.3	9.6	9.9
EU-EU trade	6.9	6.3	6.8	6.1	6.5
Common language	5.8	5.7	5.8	5.7	5.6

Notes: Estimated by OLS with 465 observations, dependent variable ln(Sxm). Absolute values of *t*-statistics are shown in parentheses below the coefficients.

negative. Since these two changes are of the same size, the net effect is that the elasticity of trade with respect to population remains about 0.7 over the five-year period, while that with respect to GDP per capita rises from 1.08 to 1.28. The coefficient estimates are significant enough that there is only a tiny probability that the population elasticity is equal to 1.0 or that the trend of the elasticity of trade with respect to GDP per capita is due to chance.

Why might producers in smaller countries concentrate more on export markets than do those in larger countries? This is not simply asking why smaller countries trade more, since that feature of geographic reality is already captured in the basic gravity model, in which trade depends on the product of the two countries' GDPs, with this amount naturally being a larger fraction of home-country GDP for smaller countries. Something more is needed to explain the further cross-sectional result showing the extra export dependence of small-country manufacturers. One possible explanation is based on the theory of optimal product mix and plant location under the assumptions of product differentiation, increasing returns to scale, and significant institutional border effects of a sort that make it more expensive for producers to enter and to supply foreign markets. Under these circumstances, there will be a trade-off for each plant designer between economies of scale in production and the greater costs of entering and servicing foreign markets. The larger the home market, the easier it will be to achieve minimum efficient scale purely on the strength of the home market, and the less likely the firm will be to rely on foreign markets. Thus the equilibrium distribution of plants and industries will be likely to show larger fractions of plant production going into exports for small countries than for large ones, to a greater extent than that implied by the basic gravity model.[9]

This kind of theoretical setup has been used to argue that the introduction of free trade arrangements will lead manufacturers to concentrate their facilities in larger countries, since facilities in larger countries have lower average costs and the lowering of border costs encourages firms to concentrate their production in the larger markets.[10] However, for any given degree of border costs, any facilities in the smaller countries will need to be more dependent on foreign markets to achieve minimum efficient plant scale. There are thus two possibilities: that all manufacturing capacity will be located in the largest countries and all foreign markets served from there, or that manufacturing will be much more

9. This point was originally made and demonstrated by Linnemann (1966). It was subsequently confirmed by Aitken (1973).

10. Head and Ries (1997a, 1997b) use a model with this structure to argue that post-FTA adjustments in Canada and the United States would show increases in the relative sizes of the U.S. industries compared to their Canadian counterparts, a conjecture that was supported by their empirical results.

widespread but with more export dependence in smaller countries. Which of these results is more likely to obtain will depend on the size and nature of the costs of servicing foreign markets and the nature of returns to scale in both production and distribution. These factors may very well differ by product and may change from one decade to another. For example, large aircraft may be in the class where returns to scale are large and the relative costs of serving unfamiliar markets small enough to leave production dominated by the country with the largest home market. Computers may once have been thought of in the same category, but the computer itself may have sufficiently reduced the optimum scale of its own production, and standardization reduced product differentiation enough, to disperse manufacture much more widely.

Patterns of OECD trade in the late 1980s and early 1990s suggest that the dispersed exporter effect, with more export reliance among the smaller countries, appears to dominate, although both the theory and empirical evidence need more careful sifting to see whether this is reflective of a broader pattern. The larger the border effects, and the greater the cost advantage of a local producer in spotting and servicing local markets, the more likely is the pattern of the late 1980s and early 1990s to be maintained. Results from the larger global sample presented in the next section may provide a first step in this direction.

Results Combining Data for OECD and Developing Countries

In this section the number of bilateral trade flows is more than doubled by adding eleven developing countries to the twenty-two-country OECD group. The increase in sample size is greater than the proportionate increase in the number of countries because the number of bilateral trade flows is equal to $n(n-1)$, where n is the total number of countries. However, the number of own-country sales figures, and hence the data available to estimate border effects, rise proportionately with the total number of countries. It actually rises slightly more than proportionately in our case, since we use bilateral trade flows for twenty-two OECD countries while having directly measured domestic sales for only sixteen. When adding new countries, however, we have included only countries for which there are published data for domestic sales of goods for at least two of the five years from 1988 through 1992. Thus the number of countries for which some data are available for the estimation of border effects rises from sixteen to twenty-seven, although there are full series for domestic sales for only six of the eleven developing countries added to the sample.

To use all of the available observations on domestic sales for the developing countries, the equation results reported in table 3-3 change the sample size each year to include all bilateral and own-country observations for which there are available observations for the current year.[11] The equation estimated is the basic gravity model, and the number of observations is generally slightly more than nine hundred. Border effects for developing countries are assessed in two ways. One is to measure border effects for the newly added countries as a group, to see if their average border effect differs systematically from the average border effect for the original group of OECD countries. This is accomplished by having two own-country sales variables, the first, OECDBORD, taking the value of 1.0 for each of the sixteen OECD countries for which own-sales data are available, and the second, DCBORD, taking the value of 1.0 for each of the additional eleven countries for which own-sales data are available in a particular year. Table 3-4 shows that forty-five of the possible fifty-five (eleven additional countries times five years) new observations of own sales are available, and shows also which are the missing observations in each year.

Results of the estimation are shown in table 3-3, along with tests of the hypothesis that the border effect is the same in the two groups of countries. The border effect is far higher in the eleven

---

11. The rule for including observations in this sample is the same as that employed in chapter 2. Any observation is excluded from the sample if the log of the dependent variable is less than 1.0. Excluding annual trade flows less than $\exp(1) = e$, or 2.7 million Canadian dollars, reduces the risk of results that are materially affected by very small trade flows that are unrepresentative of the bulk of world trade. This issue is naturally more important in the logarithmic form used here and generally for estimation of the gravity equation. Very small trade flows (less than 1 million Canadian dollars) could be represented by very large negative logarithms and could have a disproportionate influence on the least-squares results.

Table 3-3. *Basic Gravity Model of Global Trade, 1988–92*

	1988	1989	1990	1991	1992
Observations	904	899	916	910	918
Constant	4.41	4.50	4.46	4.70	5.14
	(14.6)	(14.6)	(14.4)	(15.6)	(15.7)
ln(GDPx)	0.833	0.829	0.839	0.821	0.753
	(40.9)	(40.4)	(42.3)	(42.9)	(38.6)
ln(GDPm)	0.835	0.834	0.820	0.798	0.723
	(41.9)	(41.0)	(41.5)	(41.6)	(37.3)
ln(DIST)	−0.891	−0.900	−0.903	−0.911	−0.872
	(29.8)	(29.5)	(29.9)	(31.0)	(27.3)
DCBORD	4.51	4.40	4.26	4.04	3.81
(HOME for DCs)	(13.7)	(13.2)	(12.8)	(12.0)	(8.7)
OECDBORD (HOME	2.47	2.40	2.34	2.25	2.39
for OECD)	(9.3)	(8.9)	(8.7)	(8.6)	(8.5)
$\bar{R}^2$	0.845	0.841	0.848	0.852	0.824
SEE	0.964	0.979	0.976	0.946	1.025
Border effects					
OECD	11.9	11.1	10.4	9.5	10.9
Developing countries	90.7	81.6	70.8	57.0	45.0

Notes: Estimated by OLS with dependent variable ln(Sxm). Absolute values of *t*-statistics are shown in parentheses below the coefficients. *P*-values of DC = OECD (Wald test) < .00001, except 1991 = .00001, 1992 = .00419.

additional countries, and is securely enough estimated that in the early years at least there is no statistical likelihood that the border effects are the same in the two sets of countries. There is some evidence of a falling trend in the border effect in the developing countries, both absolutely and in relation to the border effect in the OECD countries. Thus by the last year of the sample period, 1992, the probability that the two sets of border effects are the same rises to .004, compared to less than .00001 in the first three years of the sample period.

A second way of assessing the border effects in the developing countries is to allow each country to have a separately estimated border effect. Table 3-4 contains the results from that estimation, showing that the country-by-country border effects, each of which is statistically significant at a high level, are often very different. Border effects are smallest for the richest country in the group, Korea, and are much larger for some poorer countries.

Table 3-4. *Estimated Border Effects for Developing Countries*

	1988	1989	1990	1991	1992
Colombia	80.4	77.1	80.5	72.6	58.7
Ecuador	206.0	202.1	192.0	169.0	123.3
Hungary	56.6	42.2	47.7	41.0	n.a.
Korea	21.3	17.7	15.7	13.6	15.2
Myanmar	160.7	118.9	102.9	84.4	67.8
Nigeria	113.4	103.8	98.2	110.0	n.a.
Peru	124.1	112.4	136.6	n.a.	n.a.
Poland	n.a.	n.a.	61.6	48.4	n.a.
Sri Lanka	49.3	44.9	42.5	28.2	19.1
Venezuela	74.3	82.8	74.4	72.4	57.2
Zimbabwe	232.5	221.4	n.a.	n.a.	n.a.

Notes: The border effects are the antilogs of coefficients on single-observation HOME variables entered for each of the countries for which data are available in the particular year. The form of the equation is the same as in table 3-3, the only difference being that DCBORD is replaced by the separate variables for each country. The *t*-statistics on all coefficients exceed 3.0. Not available (n.a.): countries and years for which own-sales data are not available.

Next we extend the estimation to see if the model used earlier to explain the variety of border effects among the OECD countries can also explain the much larger range of experience and variety of border effects among the eleven additional countries. Remarkably, the model proves well able to explain the border effects in the developing countries, thanks principally to the variable making the border effect a function of each country's per capita income relative to the average for the whole sample of countries. Simply adding that variable to the equation shown in table 3-3 brings the coefficients on OECDBORD and DCBORD so close together that the Wald test showing the probability of the two coefficients being the same rises from essentially zero in the table 3-3 equation to a value exceeding .5 in each year and generally exceeding .75. The next step is to estimate the expanded model of table 3-2 using the data for the larger group of countries. Table 3-5 shows the results. Once again there are two variables for HOME, one (DCBORD) for the eleven additional countries and the other (OECDBORD) for the original set of sixteen OECD countries with data for domestic sales. The coefficients on DCBORD and OECDBORD are insignificantly different from one another, although there is an interesting pattern to the differences between them.

Table 3-5. *Extended Gravity Model of Global Trade, 1988–92*

	1988	1989	1990	1991	1992
Observations	904	899	916	910	918
Constant	5.00	4.40	2.34	5.04	0.33
	(2.4)	(2.1)	(1.1)	(2.5)	(0.2)
ln(GDPx)	0.943	0.947	0.918	0.897	0.772
	(32.6)	(32.4)	(33.1)	(32.0)	(28.3)
ln(GDPm)	0.920	0.911	0.873	0.833	0.709
	(34.0)	(32.6)	(32.5)	(30.9)	(26.3)
ln(DIST)	−0.720	−0.718	−0.785	−0.774	−0.826
	(15.7)	(15.2)	(16.9)	(17.1)	(16.0)
EU members	0.489	0.572	0.427	0.372	0.449
	(4.1)	(4.7)	(3.5)	(3.1)	(3.4)
Adjacent countries	0.389	0.412	0.331	0.401	0.285
	(2.4)	(2.5)	(2.0)	(2.5)	(1.6)
Common language	0.404	0.544	0.530	0.497	0.531
	(3.8)	(5.0)	(5.0)	(4.8)	(4.7)
ln(REMx)	0.016	0.115	0.169	0.046	0.286
	(0.1)	(0.7)	(1.0)	(0.3)	(1.6)
ln(REMm)	0.031	0.005	0.175	0.059	0.279
	(0.2)	(0.0)	(1.0)	(0.4)	(1.6)
DCBORD	4.11	4.00	3.61	3.56	3.03
	(7.6)	(7.0)	(6.2)	(6.1)	(4.2)
OECDBORD	3.78	3.79	3.50	3.43	3.22
	(10.8)	(10.5)	(9.4)	(9.4)	(7.2)
HOME × ln($Y/\overline{Y}$)	−0.875	−0.902	−0.840	−0.778	−0.598
	(3.7)	(3.5)	(3.1)	(2.9)	(1.7)
ln(POPx)	−0.203	−0.220	−0.165	−0.145	−0.063
	(5.7)	(6.1)	(4.7)	(4.1)	(1.7)
ln(POPm)	−0.156	−0.147	−0.107	−0.066	−0.016
	(4.7)	(4.2)	(3.2)	(1.9)	(0.4)
$\overline{R}^2$	0.859	0.857	0.860	0.861	0.834
SEE	0.922	0.928	0.939	0.918	0.998
Border effects					
DC	60.7	57.1	36.8	35.3	20.7
OECD	43.7	46.5	33.0	31.0	25.0
P-value for DC = OECD (Wald test)	.71	.75	.78	.78	.97

Notes: Estimated by OLS with dependent variable ln(Sxm). Absolute values of *t*-statistics are shown in parentheses below the coefficients.

The border effect for the developing countries is higher than that for the original set of richer countries, but is falling faster, becoming lower in 1992. Another test of the adequacy of the extended gravity model to fit the expanded group of countries is to add the full set of variables for the home country border effects for each of the additional eleven countries to an equation with a single variable for HOME, and then test whether their coefficients can individually or collectively be constrained to equal zero. Somewhat remarkably, none of the eleven additional countries has a border effect that differs significantly from the common value for the whole set of countries, once due allowance is made for the fact that the border effect varies with a country's level of per capita income.

Another interesting feature of the global sample results shown in table 3-5 is that the border effects are much larger for both the newly added countries and the original set of OECD countries. How could estimating the same model as before, with separate border effects for the two groups of countries, give higher estimates of the border effects for the original set of countries? The first and most important reason is that the border effects shown at the bottom of table 3-5 are for countries with average incomes equal to the geometric average for the thirty-three countries. This qualification is important for understanding table 3-5 because in this table, unlike tables 3-3 and 3-4, the border variable appears directly and also multiplied by each country's income relative to the average. The border effects at the bottom of table 3-5 thus show what the border effects would have been for each group of countries if they had all had the same per capita incomes, equal to the average for the group of thirty-three countries. The fact that the border effect for the developing countries starts above that for the OECD countries shows that in 1988 those countries were even more closed than their low incomes would have indicated. By 1992, on the other hand, all of the difference between the two groups of countries is explainable by the differences in the average incomes.

To show further the importance of the link between the border effects and income levels, it is possible to calculate the average border effects for the two groups of countries based on their group average incomes. The average OECD country had a border effect of 21 in 1988, falling to 14 in 1992, while the average developing country (DC) had a border effect of over 200 in 1988, falling to 63 in 1992.[12]

Even after calculating the OECD border effects at OECD-average incomes, the effects are still somewhat higher than in table 3-1. To some extent, this is a consequence of adding trading links between the OECD and the developing countries. When the sample size was increased, the number of international trade flows for each of the OECD countries rises from forty-two (imports from and exports to each of the other countries in the original sample of twenty-two) to sixty-four (two times thirty-two country pairings, since thirty-three is the total number of countries in the enlarged sample). Trade linkages among the OECD countries are tighter than those between OECD countries and the additional eleven countries, to an extent that is greater than the lower GDPs and lower average per capita incomes in the poorer countries would predict. It is also apparent from the results that the developing countries are becoming more open during the sample period, to an even greater extent than would be implied by the growth of their per capita incomes. This leads to falling average border effects for both groups of countries, with the effects falling fastest for the group of developing countries.

Comparison and Interpretation of the International Results

The average border effect for the OECD countries decreases through time in the larger sample, while it did not fall in the sample based on the trade only among the OECD countries. This difference arises because of the increasing intensity of trade linkages between the OECD and developing countries. These results show that the developing countries are globalizing much faster than the industrial countries, although starting from a much lower level of international integration.

12. These border effects are calculated as $\exp(x + y \times z)$, where x is the coefficient on the border variable, y is the coefficient on the variable $\text{HOME} \times \ln(Y/\overline{Y})$, and z is the log difference between the geometric group average income and that for the thirty-three-country sample, done separately for each group (DC and OECD) and year.

One possible implication is that the border effect for trade among the OECD countries, of about 10 for countries not linked by the EU or a common language, may represent an equilibrium based on the current state of technologies, institutions, and trading rules. If so, then the rapidly increasing openness of the developing countries might be expected to converge toward that value. This must remain conjecture until a longer sample of data becomes available and more countries are brought into the sample. Meanwhile, the estimation of any country's border effect will remain sharply dependent on the number and nature of international trading partners being used for analysis. The average border effect for OECD countries, which is about 10 when only trade with other OECD countries is considered, rises to a much higher value, subject to a falling trend, when the sample is increased by adding only a fraction of OECD trade with developing countries. If data were available for a larger fraction of the developing countries, presumably there would be an even greater estimate of the average border effect for both OECD and developing countries.

In the meantime, it would be useful to explore further the differences in border effects among developing countries, and to see to what extent they are explained by differences in economic policy strategies. For example, is it true that countries that have adopted more open trading strategies have decreased their border effects in consequence, to an extent that is greater than what would be indicated by their increases in average per capita incomes? The answer is not obvious, as policies toward openness are usually adopted because of the hoped-for positive consequences for economic growth, as discussed in chapter 6.

As already seen, there is a strong effect linking average per capita incomes to the strength of the border effect. Once this effect is allowed for, a move toward policy openness may not lead to still further reductions in the size of the border effect. Indeed, the reason for the association between per capita incomes and the size of the border effect itself needs further study. Higher incomes may simply increase the extent to which domestic consumers wish to consume foreign goods, increase their demand for income-elastic services like tourism, or otherwise alter their preferences in favor of foreign goods. On the supply side, these additional foreign contacts may increase the capacity of domestic entrepreneurs to buy from and sell into foreign markets. Alternatively, the linkages between per capita incomes and border effects may be more indirect, with higher incomes both flowing from and permitting increases in average education levels, which in turn increase the geographic range of knowledge and contacts, thus decreasing the average ignorance about life beyond national borders. This in turn would serve to decrease costs of dealing in foreign markets. In addition, to the extent that business contacts are easier and less costly to establish when there are higher levels of trust and shared values, higher levels of education may indirectly increase trade.[13] This is so because education levels are the strongest determinants of higher levels of trust and participation, thus decreasing suspicion of increased transborder engagements.[14] Finally, higher levels of income and education may themselves lie behind political support for policy changes that increase openness to international trade, capital movements, travel, and migration.

Thus disentangling the forces jointly determining policy and border effects will not be easy. In any event, it is not certain that the effects of policy changes on measured border effects will show up beyond those already identified as flowing through the channel of higher average per capita incomes. One research strategy might be to search for the effects of identified policy changes on border effects, with and without allowing for the mediating influence of changes in relative per capita incomes.[15]

Another possibility, considered later in the chapter 6 discussion of borders and growth, is that the link between per capita incomes and border effects could be reflecting in part the already established linkages between openness and growth. Alternatively, it may provide an additional channel whereby openness and per capita income levels become mutually encouraging. If so, then any event or policy that starts a convergence or catchup process in a poor

13. See, for example, Platteau (1994); Rauch (1996).
14. See Putnam (1995, 1996); Helliwell (1996c).
15. Such as, for example, the components in the Sachs and Warner (1995) index of policy openness.

country may become self-enforcing as higher incomes decrease border effects, with the increased openness then feeding back to increase growth.

Comparing the Interprovincial and International Results

Estimates of border effects comparing province-province trade with province-state trade are generally higher than those comparing domestic sales with international sales between OECD countries sharing a common language. For example, the 1992 border effect for province-state trade, for total merchandise trade is 15.2 (from table 2-2), compared to 5.6 for trade between OECD countries sharing a common language (from table 3-2).[16] Although many revisions have been made while refining both sets of estimates, this basic difference has remained. The data underlying the chapter 2 estimates are stronger, principally because there are well-founded estimates of interprovincial and province-state trade distances, while there are only assumptions available to support the data for domestic trading distances within most national economies. If the actual internal trade distances are twice as high as those calculated using the Wei procedure, then the border effects for OECD countries would rise to match those obtained from the province-state trade flows. The importance of distance for trade densities, and the implications for the estimates of the size of border effects, suggests a need for more research aimed at improving data on the geographical distribution of domestic trade flows. In the meantime, it is probably appropriate to place more weight on the evidence from the province-state trade flows, with the results for the OECD countries being taken to represent the lower end of the likely range.

16. The difference becomes larger if allowance is made for the (statistically insignificant) extent to which intraprovince trade is more intense than interprovincial trade, as shown in Helliwell (1997). In addition, the estimate for OECD countries is for those of OECD-average income per capita, and should be adjusted to account for Canada's higher-than-average per capita incomes.

Chapter 4

Prices and Capital Market Linkages

*T*HIS CHAPTER examines some price, capital market, and macro-economic evidence relating to the importance of national borders. The first section deals with prices, assessing the available evidence about the extent to which prices are more uniform within a country than across national borders, after making due allowance for the effects of distance. The second section surveys some studies that have attempted to measure and explain the apparently high degree of what is frequently referred to as "home bias" in portfolio investment—a strong revealed preference for domestic over foreign securities of otherwise equivalent attractiveness. The third section turns to macroeconomic data for an alternative set of tests of international capital market integration. This section focuses on be the literature spawned by the Feldstein-Horioka finding of high correlation between national savings and domestic investment,[1] and their inference that international capital mobility must therefore be much less than was commonly supposed.

Border Effects for Prices

If trade linkages are much tighter within than between countries, the same should be true for prices. Price differentials from one location to another motivate trade, and actual or potential movements of goods and services are the chief means of

---

1. See Feldstein and Horioka (1980).

63

limiting or eliminating price differentials between locations. The evidence leads to the conclusion that price differentials are indeed much smaller and more quickly removed within than among national economies. There are several reasons why prices may differ by location or country:[2]

—Formal trade barriers

—Transportation costs

—Trading networks that may be denser and less costly to access nearby, or within the same country[3]

—Differing consumption preferences

—Sticky prices, when measured in the currency of the country in which the good is consumed

—The presence of nontraded goods in whatever price indexes are used for comparison

One of these factors—currency fluctuations—comes into play only across national borders, while the others may apply across intranational as well as international space. Trade barriers also typically come into play only at national borders. All the other factors, which relate one way or another to the hypothesis that networks are less effective as they span larger distances and bridge larger gaps in knowledge, preferences, and institutions, are likely to come into play across national borders as well as over distance.

The first issue that can be put out of the picture is the sixth factor listed above—that departures from purchasing power parity based on aggregate price indexes are caused by the mixing of tradable goods and nontradable services. Addressing this question first is important. If the failure to observe purchasing power parity at the aggregate level were simply because prices for nontradable services are different, then it would be possible to assume that spatial and cross-border arbitrage is complete over a large range of tradable goods. However, numerous studies have shown that, while departures from purchasing power parity may be larger and longer lasting for less tradable goods and services, they are sig-

2. This is an expanded version of the list used by Engel and Rogers (1997).
3. See Rauch (1996). For an assessment of the influence of migration as a possible means of extending lower-cost networks across boundaries, see Head and Ries (1998) and chapter 5.

nificant even for the most homogeneous of traded commodities.[4] There is also evidence that the same is true within countries. Engel and Rogers found that among U.S. cities the covariability of prices is lower for goods than for services,[5] even using quite finely disaggregated data for both goods and services. They emphasize that this does not mean that goods are in fact less tradable than services, but it is the joint result of two factors—that spatial arbitrage is far from complete in either goods or services, even within the same country, and that goods' prices vary more from period to period than do service prices.

All of the listed factors, which were originally put forward as possible reasons why purchasing power parity might not hold, are also reasons why trade linkages might be denser within than between countries. Thus there is scope for research on price linkages and on trade linkages to provide mutual confirmation if similar patterns are found. Alternatively, if the two types of evidence are not consistent, then one should be more skeptical about either, or both, sets of conclusions.

Since the results in the previous chapters suggest that domestic trade linkages are far tighter than international ones, even after allowing for the effects of distance, the expected corollary for prices is that international price differentials should be greater and more long lasting than those within national borders. There is recent literature designed to test this proposition and to assess some likely reasons for the failure of the law of one price to hold either within a country or between countries. As pointed out by Engel and Rogers, the joint use of within-country and cross-country data helps to shed light on the relative importance of some mechanisms that might be in play. Their studies do this by comparing the covariability of prices among cities. Using reasoning analogous to that underlying the gravity model, they argue that costs of transport and information gathering are likely to make price linkages weaker as distance becomes greater. Since their sample includes both U.S. and Canadian cities, they are able to test whether the covariability of prices is less for cross-border city

---

4. See Isard (1977); Kravis and Lipsey (1988); Ito, Isard, and Symansky (1997).
5. See Engel and Rogers (1997).

pairs than for domestic city pairs, after allowing for the effects of distance. Engel and Rogers found that there is much more covariability of prices between pairs of cities within the same country than between Canadian and U.S. cities, after making due allowance for the effects of distance.[6] They find very large and significant border effects, so large as to far exceed the effects of distance, although the distance effects are estimated with much less precision than was possible for the trade equations estimated in chapters 2 and 3.

Parsley and Wei have found that international departures from purchasing power parity are much greater and more long lasting than are those among U.S. cities, again after making due allowance for the effects of distance.[7] A subsequent paper by Engel and Rogers shows how common costs and marketing structures within a country or region are likely to make price changes within a nation or region more closely correlated with each other than they are with price changes for similar goods in other jurisdictions.[8] In their empirical work, they study a sample of national-level consumer price indexes (CPIs) for a comparable group of commodities in thirty-two countries in North America, Europe, and Asia. Instead of national-level CPIs for the United States and Canada, they use prices for four different cities. When explaining the covariability of prices across city or country pairs, they find the biggest explanatory effect from the variability of nominal exchange rates, which of course is zero among city pairs within the same country. They find some support for the effects of distance, for tariff and nontariff barriers, and for countries being together in either Europe or North America. The three latter effects can be estimated as alternative hypotheses, each of which gets some significant support if the other two factors are ignored. When all three variables are included, nothing systematic can be found, since in Engel and Rogers's sample there is a high correlation among all the independent variables: distance, exchange rate variability, tariffs, nontariff barriers, and regional groupings. One reason for this is

6. See Engel and Rogers (1996).
7. See Parsley and Wei (1996).
8. See Engel and Rogers (1998).

that tariffs, nontariff barriers, and exchange-rate variability are all zero among city pairs in the same country, and distances are also smaller within than between regions. In the 1997 paper, Engel and Rogers were not able to test for national border effects, since the data sample did not include a sufficient number of cities within each country. Thus the best current evidence on border effects for consumer price linkages remains the earlier Engel and Rogers study based on the larger sample of U.S. and Canadian city pairs.

In summary, the evidence from prices strongly supports that from trade flows, as both types of linkage are much stronger within countries than they are between countries. It will be useful to test further to see whether the pattern of linkages by industry is similar for trade flows as it is for comparable prices.[9] Just how comparable are the current estimates of border effects from price and trade data? Engel and Rogers kindly provided me with their data to permit some initial efforts to make the results more comparable. The first step was to estimate their basic equation in logarithmic form,[10] permitting the coefficient on the border variable to be given a similar interpretation to that used in chapters 2 and 3 of this study. For the aggregate CPI, and for thirteen of the fourteen component indexes, the coefficient on the border variable was strongly significant ($t > 4.5$), although its size was generally less than half (ranging between 0.45 and 1.6) that for merchandise trade. This way of making comparisons would suggest that the border effects are smaller for prices than for merchandise trade. Engel and Rogers suggest an alternative way of assessing the size of border effects, by using a comparison of the border coefficient with the distance coefficient to compute the effect of the border as the equivalent of a certain distance. Since the distance effects in their price variability equations are far smaller and less significant than

9. Current data do not make this comparison easy, since the trade flows and prices are measured on a commodity basis, priced at the border, while the price studies have made use of components of the CPI, including all local distribution costs.

10. Engel and Rogers (1996, table 3). The data sample was also extended by Jamie Armour to increase the number of Canadian cities, hence raising the number of city pairs from 228 to 383. Since her larger sample confirmed the pattern of results in Engel and Rogers (1996), the tests reported here use the original Engel and Rogers data sample to make the results more easily comparable with their findings.

those in the merchandise trade equations, this method of comparison makes border effects much larger for prices than for merchandise trade. Because of the small size of the estimated distance effects, this procedure gives them very large and wide-ranging estimates of the width of the border.

I have since found, using their data sample, that if separate estimates are made of the distance effect for cross-border city pairs, the implied width of the border is not just large, but infinite. This is because the estimated distance effect for the cross-border city pairs takes a significant coefficient of the expected positive sign for only one of the fourteen components; it is of the wrong sign, and generally insignificant, for the aggregate and for eleven of the component prices.[11] The interpretation of this result is presumably that for the components of the CPI there are effectively no short-run price-equalizing pressures across national borders, even at the shortest distances.

How should these striking results for prices be compared to the earlier results for merchandise trade? I suspect there are two main reasons why the cross-border linkages are so weak for the price data. The first is that the prices are for components of the CPI, including many local services that are not tradable. The second is that the price variability measures used in the Engel and Rogers study are based on month-to-month changes. The cross-border measures of price variability are thus heavily influenced by short-term changes in the exchange rate between U.S. and Canadian dollars. If longer-term changes were used as the basis for comparison, or if research were based on products more similar to those entering merchandise trade and priced at the wholesale level, we might expect to find distance effects showing up more significantly in the cross-border city pairs.

---

11. This same result does not apply in the case of merchandise trade. If separate distance coefficients are estimated for domestic and cross-border merchandise trade flows, they are strongly significant and of the correct sign for all flows. Tests show that the data easily accept the constraint that the distance effects are the same for interprovincial as they are for province-state trade flows. For the price data, by contrast, the distance effects are significantly greater among the Canadian cities than they are for the transborder city pairs ($t > 2$), for the aggregate index, and for eleven of the fourteen component indexes.

Comparisons of International and Domestic Portfolio Investment

For macroeconomic analysis, the national economy has long provided the main focus of attention, with international aspects grafted on through the addition of trade and capital movements. In the case of capital market linkages, it has become increasingly common to assume full international arbitrage of yields among financial assets of similar characteristics. As Frankel and others have pointed out, this assumption runs in the face of substantial evidence that purchasing power parity is departed from in large measure and for long periods.[12] Similarly, the fact that covered interest arbitrage holds fairly closely has come to be seen as of limited importance in equalizing real returns and market interest rates in different countries, since the forward exchange rate (which is seen to be determined by the covered arbitrage process) is noticeably worse than the current spot exchange rate as a predictor of the future spot exchange rate.

In the face of such obvious departures from completely in-tegrated capital markets, there is ample scope for profitable inter-national diversification of portfolios. If national economies are distinct, then typical shares and bonds will have rates of return that are less than perfectly correlated across countries. If investors know of investment opportunities and if transaction costs are sufficiently low, then they will include foreign and domestic securities in their portfolios. Standard models of portfolio choice permit calculation of the proportion of foreign securities required in a portfolio to obtain the highest rate of return for any given degree of risk. If an actual portfolio's holdings of foreign assets are much below these values, then it is possible to conclude that domestic and foreign securities are not seen as comparable can-didates for inclusion in domestic portfolios.

The apparent preference for domestic markets applies to portfolio investment in fixed-income securities as well as equities.

12. See Frankel (1985, 1991, 1992). See also Cumby and Obstfeld (1984); Engel (1993); Frankel and Rose (1996); Froot and Rogoff (1995); Goldberg and Knetter (1997); Wei and Parsley (1995).

Frankel argues that the results for equities are especially telling, as they show that currency risk cannot be the primary reason for the revealed preference for domestic over foreign assets.[13] This is because exchange rate variation is responsible for most of the time-series variation of relative rates of return on domestic versus foreign fixed-income securities, while this is not so for equity returns, which follow much different paths in separate national markets. Equities thus provide a much greater incentive for variance-reducing international portfolio diversification. Frankel also shows that if there is a strong home-country preference for domestically produced goods, risk-averse domestic investors may not need a very large share of their fixed-income investment in foreign securities to obtain an optimal degree of portfolio diversification.[14] This leaves unanswered the issue of why there should be such a preference for domestic products, the question addressed in previous chapters, but does suggest that the home preference for fixed-income securities may provide supporting evidence for the home preference for goods and services without adding to either the nature or the size of the overall puzzle.

Equity markets provide a more dramatic example of the importance of national borders, as many studies have shown that standard models of portfolio diversification imply that investors have far less than optimal proportions of their assets invested abroad. For example, pension plans in seven major industrial countries held on average 92 percent of their portfolios (comprising both stocks and bonds) in domestic assets.[15] In each case, the proportion held in domestic assets was much higher than the country's share of total world stock and bond markets. Thus U.S. pension portfolios held 4 percent of their portfolios in foreign assets, while foreign markets comprised two-thirds of the global equities market and 60 percent of the global bond market. U.K. pension funds were the most internationally diversified, with 26 percent of their assets invested abroad. However, this still means that 74 percent is invested in domestic assets, while a fully diversified portfolio would have

13. See Frankel (1994, p. 11).
14. See Frankel (1994, p. 11).
15. See Jorion (1994).

something closer to the U.K.'s share of global bond and equity supply (2 percent of bonds and 10 percent of equities) invested at home.[16]

A study by Tesar and Werner is especially helpful in comparing gross trading and net holdings of assets across country pairs.[17] Their study is unusual in being able to combine data on rates of return with data on portfolio allocations. They argue that this allows them to show more conclusively that investors put more of their funds into domestic assets than they would if they were investing to obtain the highest rate of return for a given level of risk. They find that home preference for equities is higher than for goods, as suggested by portfolio holdings of foreign assets that are much smaller than merchandise exports as shares of final sales. Tesar and Werner also show that country pairs differ in their intensity of shareholdings and in their propensity to trade or "churn" their holdings. For most of the country pairs, foreign holdings are traded more actively than domestic holdings, leading Tesar and Werner to conclude that the low holdings of foreign equities cannot be explained by high transaction costs in foreign markets.

Other studies have considered a variety of reasons why investors might prefer to hold such high proportions of their portfolios in domestic assets.[18] The general conclusion is that, while capital is free to move among at least the industrial economies, investors prefer to invest in their own countries. This is consistent with the results for merchandise trade. For securities, just as for goods, the perceived advantages of dealing within familiar and trusted networks, institutions, and markets are greater than the potential gains from further international diversification. The evidence that portfolios are becoming more internationally diversified as global trading becomes more accessible needs to be interpreted in the light of the strongly domestic focus of current holdings. Over the

16. Bottazzi, Pesenti, and van Wincoop (1996) show that a negative correlation between wage and nonwage returns might support some degree of home-country bias, although nothing like the actual preference for home securities.

17. See Tesar and Werner (1994).

18. See Baxter and Jermann (1997); French and Poterba (1991); Gordon and Bovenberg (1996); Lewis (1995); Pesenti and van Wincoop (1996); Uppal (1992).

past twenty years, reductions in border controls and taxes have been even greater for securities transactions than for merchandise trade. For certain classes of securities, especially assets denominated in the same currency but sold in different countries, differences in rates of return have narrowed substantially.[19] There has been a parallel but partial erosion of the size of border effects in securities markets.[20] Reductions in capital controls have no doubt played an important role in increasing the international scope of securities markets, but the still pervasively domestic composition of port-folios suggests that the border effects involve a subtle combination of information networks, national systems of accounting and regulation, and assessments of foreign risks that are often poorly grounded. The weak basis of information for the assessment of the riskiness of foreign markets and institutions makes those assess-ments likely to change rapidly whenever the credibility or pros-pects of foreign markets are called into question.

Macroeconomic Evidence: The Feldstein-Horioka Paradox

The line of research initiated by Feldstein and Horioka provides another strand of evidence against the assumption of unified global capital markets.[21] Feldstein and Horioka argued that if capital markets were truly integrated, then there would be only slight correlations between national savings rates and domestic investment rates, since savers would invest their funds where returns were highest, with no special preference for local markets. They found, however, that savings and investment rates are highly correlated across countries, leading them to conclude that national capital markets are far from being fully integrated. Later research showed that such correlations could be consistent with full capital market integration, under suitable assumptions about the patterns of shocks and the nature of the business cycle.[22] Further work by

19. See Marston (1995) for an extensive survey.
20. For a review of the recent evidence, see Tesar and Werner (1998).
21. See Feldstein and Horioka (1980).
22. Theoretical models assuming full mobility of capital and displaying positive correla-tions between national savings and domestic investment have been developed by Baxter and

Feldstein and others has tended to support their initial interpretation, although with the qualification that the strength of the correlations falls on a decade-by-decade basis, consistent with the assumption that capital markets are becoming increasingly integrated.[23] However, studies of savings and investment correlations over much longer periods reveal that much, if not all, of the increases in capital mobility in the second half of the twentieth century, at least as measured by Feldstein-Horioka–type correlations, has been only a recovery of capital mobility lost during the first half of the century.[24]

If data are available for savings and investment for subnational economies, then a comparison of the savings and investment correlations among subnational regions with those among countries should provide a more direct test of the Feldstein-Horioka hypothesis. The Canadian provincial accounts are complete enough to permit the tests to be done on a comprehensive basis, and to permit the interprovincial correlations to be estimated in tandem with those among the Organization for Economic Cooperation and Development (OECD) countries. Table 4-1 shows results comparing interprovincial and international capital mobility.[25] The main equation estimated is an extension of the Feldstein-Horioka procedure in several ways. The original Feldstein and Horioka results were pure cross sections, with one observation per country. Others have argued that there are many ways in which the structures of national economies might differ so as to lead some countries to have higher national savings and domestic investment rates, even if capital mobility among countries were indeed perfect. One way of dealing with this issue, proposed by Fujiki and

---

Crucini (1993), Engel and Kletzer (1989), Finn (1990), Obstfeld (1986), and Tesar (1991), among others. Multicountry empirical models that embody perfect capital mobility also show positive correlations between savings and investment when subjected to changes in government spending (Bryant and others, 1988). Coakley, Kulasi, and Smith (1996) argue that current account solvency will tend to make current account imbalances average out over the long run.

23. See Armstrong, Balasubramanyam, and Salisu (1996); Dooley, Frankel, and Mathieson (1987); Feldstein (1994); Feldstein and Bacchetta (1991); Jansen and Schulze (1996); Murphy (1984); Obstfeld (1995); Obstfeld and Taylor (1997); Taylor (1994).

24. See Taylor (1996a, 1996b).

25. The table is based on results reported in Helliwell and McKitrick (1998).

Table 4-1. *Comparing Provincial and National Border Effects for Savings*

	Equation			
	(i)	(ii)	(iii)	(iv)
Observations	621	27	27	27
Estimation method	SUR fixed effects	OLS	OLS	OLS
Dependent variable	I_{it}	I_i	I_i	I_i
Data period	Annual 1961–93	Averaged 1961–93	Averaged 1961–71	Averaged 1983–93
Constants	Each i and t			
Coefficients				
b: Savings	0.268	0.780	0.718	0.670
	(3.8)	(4.3)	(3.5)	(4.9)
c: Savings(DPROV)	−0.29	−0.850	−0.830	−0.691
	(2.8)	(4.5)	(3.9)	(4.9)
P-value of Wald test of equality of the two coefficients	.18	.10	.05	.26
$\bar{R}^2$	0.43	0.53	0.51	0.53
SEE	.041	.027	.036	.022

Notes: The data sources are described in Helliwell and McKitrick (1998). The results reported include all provinces. That paper shows that removing Newfoundland, the major outlier, significantly raises the goodness of fit but does not alter the size and offsetting pattern of the savings retention coefficients. The results above treat transfers received as income to the recipient province and not as saving by contributing provinces. Alternative assumptions do not alter the results. The fixed-effects results in equation (i) are two-way, in that they include separate intercepts for each country or province, as well as for each year. One-way fixed-effects estimates, without including year effects, give a larger negative estimate for *c,* and a higher probability that the sum of $b + c = 0$. The savings and investment rates are measured annually in equation (i), but are averages spanning the 1961–93 period in equation (ii), 1961–71 in equation (iii), and 1983–93 in equation (iv).

Kitamura, is to pool time-series and cross-section data and then allow for country-specific fixed effects.[26] They find that for samples based on OECD data this gives a smaller estimate of the parameter *b* measuring the partial effect of a change in national savings on the domestic investment rate. Our application extends the Fujiki and Kitamura procedure further, in a way that allows a precise test of the relative importance of national borders. We do this by extending our data sample to include comparably measured annual savings and investment rates from 1961 through 1993 for seventeen OECD countries (not including Canada) and ten Canadian provinces. We then augment the specification to include a separate

26. See Fujiki and Kitamura (1995).

slope term for the provincial observations. The equation estimated is thus the following:

$$I_{it} = a_i + b(S_{it}) + c(\text{DPROV})(S_{it}) + d_t + e_{it} \qquad (4\text{-}1)$$

where I_{it} is fixed public and private capital expenditures as a share of GDP for country or province i and year t; the a_i are a set of fixed-effects constant terms, one for each country or province; S_{it} is the annual saving rate in each country or province; DPROV is a variable taking the value 1.0 for each observation representing a province; the d_t are estimates of year-specific fixed effects; and the e_{it} are error terms assumed to be randomly distributed. The coefficient b is the savings retention rate estimated by Feldstein and Horioka and many others. It is normally found to be positive and significantly different from zero, leading to the inference that capital markets are not fully integrated. The results of estimating equation (4-1) are shown as equation (i) in table 4-1. Also shown, for comparison, are three estimates of the basic Feldstein-Horioka cross-sectional regression: equation (ii) using averaged data for the entire 1961–93 period, and the others using subsample averages from the beginning and end of the data range, 1961–71 as equation (iii) and 1983–93 as equation (iv).

As already noted, there are several reasons why a positive relationship between savings and investment rates might exist even if capital markets were fully integrated, the principal one being that goods markets also need to be highly integrated if an increase in savings in one country is to be transferred seamlessly to another country for investment. There was a long-standing literature on what was in the 1920s known as the "transfer problem," which considered what was necessary to permit savings in one country to be transferred in real terms to another country. In the original context, the problem related to post–World War I reparations payments, but there is a clear implication for any exogenous increase in savings and its transfer to investment in another country. At one extreme, if the saving takes place in terms of a commodity, and if that commodity is also transportable and useful as capital equipment, and if the saver wishes to invest abroad, then the asset can simply be moved to another country, put in place, and set to work. Saving in one country thereby becomes investment in another. But what if the saving takes the form of purchasing power in the domestic currency? How can this purchasing power be transferred to become a factory in another country? Even if financial assets in different countries are seen as very close substitutes, and can be exchanged at low cost from holders in one country to holders in another country, more is required to effect the transfer of real resources from one country to another. If the country with the increased savings is to effect the transfer, it needs to achieve a current account surplus. If there is a simultaneous demand for investment goods arising across the same border, as in the example above, then the problem is solved, but generally this is not the case. Hence there generally need to be changes in relative prices and real exchange rates sufficient to induce a current account surplus in the high-saving country. The price flexibility required to achieve this requires high integration of goods markets, hence the increasing recognition that the savings retention coefficient reflects national separation of some combination of markets for goods and capital.[27]

Thus, although a finding of a significant positive value for b does not imply immobility of capital, it does imply immobility of some combination of goods and capital. This brings us to the interpretation of the coefficient c applicable to provincial savings rates. If this coefficient is zero, then Canadian provinces and OECD countries are similar in their investment responses to innovations in saving. If c is positive, then savings retention is greater for provinces than for countries, an unlikely finding given the high retention previously found for national savings in OECD countries. If c is negative, this implies that savings retention is less for provinces than for OECD countries, with the net savings retention calculated as the sum of the two coefficients. Thus if b and c are of equal size and opposite sign, and both significant, then the conclusion would be that national borders set limits to the transfer of savings, while provincial boundaries do not. This would provide a strong confirmation of Feldstein and Horioka's interpretation of their

27. Bosworth (1995), in his review of a volume of studies of capital mobility, notes that the literature by now recognizes, after perhaps a too-lengthy lag, that a zero value for the savings retention coefficient requires full integration of markets for goods as well as capital.

results, since many of the reasons used by others to explain away the Feldstein-Horioka results imply that savings and investment rates should be correlated across provinces as well as across countries.

What do the results show? The estimates of b and c are both significant, of almost identical size, and of opposite sign, implying a significant savings retention effect for national borders, but none for provincial borders. The estimated value of b in equation (i) is lower than in many of the earlier studies based on pure cross sections, but is in line with other estimates, such as those of Fujiki and Kitamura,[28] that also use fixed-effects estimators with panel data to estimate savings retention. Ours is the first study to pool provincial and national data, so no direct comparison is available on that score. However, Bayoumi and Klein compare the provincial data with those for the OECD countries, and find results consistent with ours. Dekle uses cross-sectional data for forty-seven Japanese prefectures and finds no savings retention among them; a finding consistent with our results for the Canadian provinces.[29] Sinn, using more fragmentary data for regional accounts in the United States, also finds no evidence of savings retention among regions.[30] Equation (ii) uses a pure cross section of the same sort employed by Feldstein and Horioka, and finds a savings retention coefficient of 0.78 for the OECD countries, offset by a slightly larger provincial effect. Equations (iii) and (iv) show that the savings retention rate for the OECD countries was higher in the 1960s (0.718) than in the late 1980s and early 1990s (0.577), replicating the slight downward trend found in some other studies. However, in each case the OECD effect is offset by a provincial border effect of equal size, so that provincial savings retention remains essentially zero in all time periods, whether

28. See Fujiki and Kitamura (1995).

29. See Dekle (1996). Actually, Dekle finds negative savings retention using total savings, and a zero value for b using private savings and private investment. He interprets the negative coefficient using the total data as a result of government taxing and spending policies that distribute public investment in such a way as to favor poorer regions, which also have lower savings rates. See also Yamori (1995).

30. See Sinn (1992). This finding pointing to domestic capital mobility was also confirmed by Bayoumi and Rose (1993), who found no correlation of savings and investment across regions in the United Kingdom.

estimated using cross sections based on averaged data or with panel data allowing for country and province fixed effects.

Evidence from studies of savings and investment thus strongly confirms that the internal structure of national markets is far denser and more fluid than that of the global market. Internal markets for capital and goods are closely enough linked that savings arising in one province are as likely to be invested in one province as in any other. For national economies, by contrast, changes in savings are much more likely to be accompanied by changes in investment in the same country. Patterns of savings-investment correlations are thus consistent with studies of international portfolio composition. Both reveal a strong preference for national assets, adding to the evidence from prices and trade flows that internal economic linkages are far tighter than those across national boundaries.

Chapter 5

Borders and Migration

How IMPORTANT are national borders as determinants of migration patterns? Have these border effects grown or shrunk, and what are their causes and implications? The evidence is mixed. On the one hand, citizenship is now much harder to get, and migration much more regulated, than was the case a century ago. On the other hand, a much greater fraction of a far larger world population now has enough knowledge and resources to move to another country, whether for tourism or settlement. So some costs of migration have risen, while others have fallen.

It is useful to summarize the evidence on the patterns of migration, both internal and between countries, to see if any judgments can be drawn about the net effect of national borders on the extent of migration. The main empirical results presented in this book compare the fluidity of internal and international migration, using methods similar to those employed already to measure the relative strength of domestic and international trade linkages.

The study of migration has long relied on the same gravity equation that has been used to explain trade flows. In both cases, the empirical dominance of the gravity model was not at first matched by well-articulated theories to explain its success. In the case of trade, the empirical success is now more widely accepted, because almost all trade theories take a gravity form under a wide range of conditions. In migration studies, there have been fewer attempts to ground the gravity form in explicit theories of migration, and to some extent there is still seen to be a contrast between "gravity" and "economic" models of migration.[1] In trade, by contrast, the gravity form is seen as implied by most of the alternative economic models of trade. There is every reason to expect that the same process will eventually take place to strengthen the theoretical reputation of the gravity model of migration. Meanwhile, surveys of the empirical literature and the equations reported here continue to be consistent with the gravity model in finding strong effects of distance as a deterrent to migration.

The puzzle posed by the empirical results, at least as viewed by many researchers, has been that the estimated negative effects of distance on migration are far greater than could be accounted for by reasonable estimates of the direct costs of moving. The inference is that there must be other reasons for nonmigration that are correlated with distance, the key candidates being benefits from migration that are small and increasingly unknown as distance increases, psychic costs of moving that increase with distance, and reductions in the quality and amount of information as distance increases.[2]

More recent research, based on both internal and international migration, has added a fourth candidate: the networks of contacts and support based on past migration flows. For example, it has been found that the northward flows of black migrants from southern to northern states in the United States kept growing long after the returns to such migration had passed their peaks. This puzzle has been explained by the declining costs of migration for those who followed the paths blazed by others and replanted their roots in communities in which they had many connections based on previous flows of family and friends.[3] Similar reasoning explains the strong clustering effects of domestic and international migrations, with people coming from the same town in one country ending up together in another country halfway around the globe.

---

1. For example, a recent survey by Gallup (1997) makes a distinction between the gravity model and a range of theories of individual migration decisionmaking based on economic considerations.

2. See Greenwood (1975, p. 398).

3. See Carrington, Detragiache, and Vishwanath (1996).

The various reasons for the large effects of distance on migration also have implications for the likely effects of borders, since we have already found, or at least inferred, that many of the networks of knowledge, institutions, and shared values that tend to facilitate trade are at least partly determined by national borders. To the extent that networks supporting trade and migration are alike, and are similarly affected by distance and national boundaries, we would expect to find border effects for trade and migration that have similar patterns and sizes. There is a chicken-and-egg problem, of course, since any past distribution of migrants will tend to determine future ones, and borders themselves may originally be chosen to reflect preexisting lines of cleavage among linguistic, ethnic, religious, or cultural groups whose members may for other reasons always have been less likely to migrate to the other's region.

Along with the strong reasons for expecting border effects to have similar patterns for trade and for migration, there are also grounds for expecting differences. The primary reason for difference relates to the much greater role for national border policies influencing migration. Although it is true that national borders are where tariffs and trade restrictions come into play, and that they also serve as boundary lines for the main use areas for national currencies, in the second half of the twentieth century movements of population have been more restricted than those of goods and services. There have also been differing trends, and large reductions in tariffs and nontariff barriers have not been matched by corresponding easing of restrictions on international migration. Internal migration, by contrast, has been much less the focus for policy decisions, and in most countries is not subject to any restrictions.

The high profile of international migration policy, and the general absence of domestic migration policies, may help to explain the major differences in the literature relating to international and internal migration. The study of internal migration, especially in the United States, has chiefly focused on the migration decision, with much less study of the consequences of migration, especially for the populations of the receiving regions.[4] By

4. See the survey by Greenwood (1975).

contrast, the recent study of international migration concentrates on the consequences of migration, especially for the fortunes of the migrants themselves and the residents of the countries and cities to which the migrants move.[5] While the earlier literature on the "brain drain" analyzed the costs and benefits of migration chiefly from the point of view of the countries from which the migrants came,[6] most recent studies of international migration assess the costs and benefits chiefly from the viewpoint of the receiving country. This may be partly because the receiving countries are where most of the social science research is done. Probably more important is the fact that the key limits to migration are set by the immigration policies of the receiving countries rather than the emigration policies of the source countries.

In this chapter, the intent is not to study either the motivations of the migrants or the costs and benefits of migration policies, but rather to compare the densities of internal and international migration flows, and hence to derive benchmark estimates of border effects for migration. The basic tool used is the gravity model, with the mass measured by population and distance measured the same way as for the trade equations in chapters 2 and 3. Economic incentives to migrate are chiefly captured by per capita income levels in the source and destination provinces, states, or countries. To provide the most comparable and complete data for provinces, states, and nations, the basic measures of migration will be taken from periodic censuses, which in most countries report results by state or province of current residence, and report the place of birth for each individual. Typically, and especially in Canada and the United States, the places of birth are reported as a state or province if the individual was born in the same country, or by country if born in another country. To make the gravity model of migration match that for province-state trade, it would have been much preferable if U.S.-born Canadian residents had been asked for their states of birth, and if Canadian-born U.S. residents had been asked their provinces of birth. They were not, so the sample size must be reduced accordingly.

5. As surveyed by Borjas (1994, 1995b).
6. See Bhagwati and Rodriguez (1975).

More specifically, the main results reported here are based on the Canadian census data for 1991 and the U.S. census for 1990. We shall start with separate models based in turn on the Canadian and U.S. census data, and then attempt to compare the two.

Taking the Canadian model first, the dependent variable is a measure of cumulative immigration. The number of residents in each province is split by place of birth: the same province, each of the other provinces, or the United States. No data are available on when the migration took place; it may have occurred at any time between the date of birth and the census date. The independent variables, following the basic structure of the gravity model, are the logs of population in the source and destination jurisdictions, the log of distance between the two, the border variable HOME taking the value of 1.0 for each migration flow from one part to another of the same country, and finally, to represent the economic incentives for migration, the average (taken from 1961 to 1989) log per capita real personal incomes in the source (Yx) and destination (Ym) jurisdictions:

$$\ln(\mathrm{MIG}xm) = \alpha_0 + \alpha_1\ln(\mathrm{POP}x) + \alpha_2\ln(\mathrm{POP}m) + \alpha_3\ln(\mathrm{DIST}xm)$$
$$+ \alpha_4\mathrm{HOME} + \alpha_5\ln(Yx) + \alpha_6\ln(Ym) + \varepsilon_{xm} \qquad (5\text{-}1)$$

In some equations, we also include measures of the attractiveness of alternative destinations of the sort proposed by Feder, and Foot and Milne, and tested earlier in the context of gravity models for trade.[7] Initial results of adding long averages of unemployment rates did not reveal any improvement in the explanation based solely on differentials in per capita personal incomes, despite the evidence from net interprovincial migration equations that per capita incomes and relative unemployment rates both have significant roles to play.[8] Using annual net interstate migration data for the United States, Treyz and others split per capita income differentials into three component ratios: relative incomes for employed workers in given industries, the industry-based relative wage mix for each state, and the relative probability of being employed, as measured by each state's employment ratio relative

7. See Feder (1980); Foot and Milne (1984).
8. See Helliwell (1996a).

to the national average.[9] For cumulative effects, they found that the relative wage and industry mix effects were similar, while the employment opportunity effect was about 50 percent larger than that for the wages of employed workers. In our equations, the use of personal incomes per capita combines the employment and wage effects, thus constraining them to have the same coefficient. This is more likely to be suitable for cumulative migration, which is the focus of our attention, than it might be for annual migration flows. The risk of failing to find a job, which constrains migrants from moving to regions of relatively high unemployment, may merge with the relative wage differential over the longer term when cyclical differences in regional unemployment rate differentials are averaged out. This may help to explain why in the Canadian equations there is no additional effect from the unemployment rates on cumulative migration, once average per capita incomes are included, even though such effects were present in earlier studies based on annual net migration flows.

The results for Canada are shown in table 5-1. Equations (i)–(iii) show the results for the ninety observations on interprovincial migration, and equations (iv)–(vi) show the effect of adding migration from the United States to each of the ten Canadian provinces. Most equations also include a variable covering all migration to and from Quebec. Adding this variable materially improves the overall fit of the model, because there is much less migration to and from Quebec than among the other provinces. Subsidiary test results indicate that the lower propensity for migration to and from Quebec is of equal strength for movements from Quebec to other provinces, from other provinces to Quebec, and for movements from the United States to Quebec.[10]

The explanatory power of the gravity model of migration is high, the coefficients are all of the right sign and highly significant, and the implied border effect is as shown at the bottom of the

9. See Treyz and others (1993).

10. To see whether the effects were equal for Quebec immigration and emigration, and for interprovincial and international migration, the Quebec variable was split into its three component parts, and a test was run to see if the coefficients were equal. The P-value of the equality restriction was .47, thus indicating no significant difference among the three effects.

Table 5-1. *Interprovincial and U.S.-Province Migration*

				Equation		
	(i) Canada	*(ii)* Canada	*(iii)* Canada	*(iv)* Canada + United States	*(v)* Canada + United States	*(vi)* Canada + United States
Observations	90	90	90	100	100	100
Estimation method	OLS	OLS	OLS	OLS	OLS	OLS
Dependent variable ln(MIG*xm*)	Inter-province	Inter-province	Inter-province	Inter-province + United States	Inter-province + United States	Inter-province + United States
Constant	4.11	−1.87	1.05	0.97	−6.58	−3.85
	(2.7)	(1.4)	(0.6)	(0.5)	(4.1)	(1.9)
ln(POP*x*)	0.588	1.00	0.984	0.592	0.994	0.978
	(5.4)	(10.8)	(10.8)	(5.6)	(10.7)	(10.6)
ln(POP*m*)	0.200	0.617	0.618	0.223	0.625	0.624
	(1.8)	(6.6)	(6.8)	(2.2)	(7.0)	(7.0)
ln(DIST)	−0.937	−0.992	−1.06	−0.922	−0.977	−1.04
	(11.2)	(16.2)	(16.2)	(11.3)	(15.9)	(15.7)
ln(*Yx*)	−0.01	−2.00	−2.08	−0.05	−1.98	−2.07
	(0.0)	(3.5)	(3.5)	(0.1)	(3.5)	(3.5)
ln(*Ym*)	6.39	4.40	4.06	6.11	4.18	3.91
	(8.9)	(7.7)	(6.9)	(9.2)	(7.6)	(6.9)
ln(RPOP*x*)	. . .	. . .	0.267	. . .	. . .	0.251
			(1.5)			(1.4)
ln(RPOP*m*)	. . .	. . .	0.439	. . .	. . .	0.370
			(2.4)			(2.1)
HOME	. . .	. . .	. . .	2.79	4.58	4.43
				(5.8)	(11.0)	(10.7)
QUEBEC	. . .	−1.42	−1.26	. . .	−1.37	−1.23
		(8.6)	(7.3)		(8.5)	(7.2)
$\bar{R}^2$	0.854	0.922	0.926	0.854	0.917	0.920
SEE	0.649	0.474	0.461	0.636	0.477	0.469
Border effect	. . .	. . .	. . .	16.2	97.1	84.1

Note: Absolute values of *t*-statistics are shown in parentheses below the coefficients.

table. In equation (v), the border effect answers the following question: For every resident in a Canadian province who was born in a U.S. state, how many other residents of that province will there be who were born in some other Canadian province (excluding Quebec) of similar size, distance, and personal income per capita? The current answer is close to one hundred. These border effects for migration are high enough to be consistent with high border effects for goods, and high enough also to make it reasonable to suppose that at the margin interprovincial migration is much less likely than is international migration to open new doors for trade.

The results for the corresponding model of migration for U.S. states are shown in table 5-2. The estimates are based on data for fifty states plus the District of Columbia, rather than the thirty large states covered by the trade model, since initial tests of the migration model using data for the thirty states showed much weaker results than those obtained for Canadian interprovincial migration. In particular, the initial U.S. results showed less significant effects of relative incomes than was apparent for Canadian interprovincial migration. This may reflect genuine differences between the two countries in the determinants of cumulative regional migration, as other studies have shown uneven migratory responses to interstate income differences. For example, Barro and Sala-i-Martin show an apparent effect of a state's income level on its net immigration from other states as being one-third as large in the 1980s as in the 1950s, although the effect is statistically significant in both cases.[11] Sherwood-Call examines net migration flows for the forty-eight continental states in five-year periods and finds a strongly negative correlation between cross-sectional differences among states in 1975 per capita incomes and net migration over the five following years.[12] From 1955 to 1960, by contrast, there were significant net migration flows from the states with lower to higher 1955 per capita incomes. She argues that the reason for the decline in the apparent effect of per capita income levels on subsequent migration is that by the 1970s the century-long convergence among state income levels had run its course,

11. See Barro and Sala-i-Martin (1995).
12. See Sherwood-Call (1996).

Table 5-2. *Interstate and Canada-State Migration*

	(i) United States	(ii) United States	(iii) United States	(iv) United States + Canada	(v) United States + Canada	(vi) United States + Canada
				Equation		
Observations	2,548	2,548	2,548	2,599	2,599	2,599
Estimation method	OLS	OLS	OLS	OLS	OLS	OLS
Dependent variable ln(MIGxm)	Interstate	Interstate	Interstate	Interstate + Canada	Interstate + Canada	Interstate + Canada
Constant	−21.3	−20.4	−18.6	−23.7	−22.6	−20.8
	(13.9)	(14.9)	(13.7)	(15.4)	(16.5)	(15.3)
ln(POPx)	0.748	0.738	0.738	0.749	0.739	0.738
	(42.0)	(46.1)	(46.8)	(41.9)	(46.0)	(46.7)
ln(POPm)	0.808	0.852	0.789	0.806	0.851	0.787
	(45.3)	(53.2)	(45.6)	(45.6)	(53.5)	(45.8)
ln(DIST)	−0.703	−0.968	−0.980	−0.694	−0.964	−0.976
	(31.0)	(40.3)	(41.3)	(30.7)	(40.1)	(40.2)
ln(Yx)	0.178	0.077	0.075	0.174	0.079	0.077
	(1.5)	(0.7)	(0.7)	(1.5)	(0.7)	(0.7)
ln(Ym)	1.14	0.260	0.242	1.18	0.294	0.276
	(9.6)	(2.3)	(2.2)	(10.0)	(2.6)	(2.5)
ln(RPOPx)	...	0.485	0.501	...	0.480	0.496
		(6.0)	(6.2)		(5.9)	(6.2)
ln(RPOPm)	...	2.08	1.90	...	2.10	1.91
		(25.6)	(22.9)		(25.8)	(23.1)
HOME	...	...	...	1.95	1.88	1.88
				(14.5)	(15.6)	(15.8)
SUN	...	...	0.816	...	...	0.824
			(8.8)			(9.0)
$\bar{R}^2$	0.690	0.753	0.760	0.686	0.750	0.758
SEE	0.905	0.807	0.795	0.907	0.809	0.797
Border effect	...	...	...	7.0	6.5	6.5

Notes: Absolute values of *t*-statistics are shown in parentheses below the coefficients.

and that the remaining income differences, despite being of substantial size, reflected an equilibrium in which the higher incomes were compensation for other less attractive features of the quality of life. This in itself would not give rise to the significant movement away from the richer states in the late 1970s, which she attributes to changes in the fortunes of the richer states, with their slower growth leading to out-migration even though their income levels remained higher than average.

Before comparing the results for the Canadian and U.S. migration equations, it is useful to compare the raw data. In the United States, 60 percent of the respondents were born in the state in which they were residing when the 1990 census was taken. For Canada, 72 percent of respondents were born in the province in which they resided when the 1991 census was taken. Although this suggests higher U.S. internal mobility, the figures have to be somehow adjusted to reflect the fact that the U.S. states are closer together than are Canadian provinces. In both the Canadian and U.S. results, increasing distance reduces cumulative migration by almost the same proportion. Simple comparisons are made difficult by the fact that in both countries there are slightly populated states at great distances from the rest: Hawaii and Alaska in the United States, and Newfoundland in Canada. Simple average distances among states are 1,226 miles for the United States, compared to 1,194 miles for interprovincial distances in Canada. This gap would not be enough to offset the difference between the stay-at-home proportions reported above.

Simple measures are also possible for population flows between the two countries. If income levels were equal, the gravity model would predict balanced population flows between the two countries. In fact, there were three times more 1990 U.S. residents who had been born in Canada than there were Canadian residents born in the United States—745,000 compared to 249,000.[13] Thus we would expect to find larger border effects in the Canadian equation than in the U.S. equation. What do the results show?

The estimates of the border effects in Canada are somewhat sensitive to the specification of the equation, while the U.S. results are less sensitive. However, whatever specification is used, the border effects are significant in both countries, while being ten or more times higher for Canada than for the United States. As

13. University of Toronto, Computing in the Humanities and Social Sciences Data Centre, http://datacentre.utoronto.ca:5680/cgi-bin/census/censcgi.sh; Bureau of the Census (1990).

already noted, for migration among the anglophone provinces, compared to migration from the United States to Canada, the border effect is almost 100. In the United States, however, the density of cumulative interstate migration is about seven times greater than cumulative migration from Canada, after adjusting for differences in distances, income levels, and population.

Another difference between the Canadian and U.S. results remains the much greater influence of relative incomes in triggering interprovincial rather than interstate migration. Perhaps this indicates, as Sherwood-Call has suggested, that current interstate income differences in the United States reflect compensating differentials. If this is true to a greater extent for the United States than for Canada, then this would help to explain the larger estimated effect of income differentials in the Canadian case. In both countries, income in the target location for migration has more influence than income in the source province or state. For the United States, both estimated effects are much smaller than for Canada, and income in the source state is of the wrong sign, although insignificantly so. To see whether the well-documented Sunbelt migration is influencing the estimated income effects, equations (iii) and (vi) in table 5-2 add a variable reflecting migration from a state, or from Canada, to California and Florida. These destinations were chosen because they were the largest outliers in equations (ii) and (v), and are the largest recipients of pre- and postretirement migration to the Sunbelt. Although the variable is very significant, its inclusion does not alter either the income effect or the estimate of the border effect. In general, adding the migrants from Canada to the U.S. interstate migration equation has little effect on the estimated parameters, as long as the border variable is included to allow for the sevenfold border effect.

One feature common to the models of both countries is the strong overall support for the gravity model, with strongly estimated effects of distance and of the populations of source and destination states or provinces. The coefficients on source and destination population are almost identical for the United States, while for Canada the coefficient on destination population is smaller. This suggests that for Canada, compared to the United

States, internal migration is less drawn toward the provinces with the largest current populations. Adding variables measuring the remoteness of alternative destinations improves the fit of both models. The current results are defined using a weighted average measure of distance divided by population, calculated separately for the source and destination regions. Since the variables measure the remoteness of other sources and destinations, they are expected to take positive coefficients in the equations explaining cumulative bilateral migration, and do so. There is some evidence, in the Canadian case, that the equation would be improved by the use of a measure that also included income levels in other sources and destinations, in the constrained way used previously by Feder. This is less likely in the case of the U.S. equation, given the weak direct effect of relative incomes on cumulative bilateral migration among U.S. states and from Canada to the United States.

Subsequent research is needed to consider the effects that migration is likely to have on merchandise and service trade, and on the institutions and social capital of the source and destination countries. Some studies have suggested that migration does bring increased trade in its wake, with the evidence being stronger for imports from the source country than for exports from the destination country.[14] Social and cultural differences are perhaps even harder to measure reliably than are economic differences, since the measures used may be even more culture-specific. The links between borders and social differences are important enough to make some effort worthwhile. The existing evidence suggests that differences in various measures of what has come to be called "social capital," or aspects of the civic society, are large and long-standing among countries, and among regions and social groupings within nations. Rice and Feldman established that migrants bring social capital with them, and that these attitudes tend to be durable over several generations.[15] There is also evidence that

14. See Gould (1994); Head and Ries (1998); Rauch (1996). Helliwell (1997) presents some evidence suggesting that international migration has larger trade effects than does interprovincial migration, as might be expected if the international differences in institutions were much greater than the interprovincial ones. Interprovincial information flows are also likely to be smoother than their international equivalents.

15. See Rice and Feldman (1995).

where migrants gather together in separate communities their attitudes and behavior converge more slowly toward the averages in the regions or communities in which they live.[16]

It is argued in chapter 7 that national institutions and networks offer the possibility that transaction costs should be lower within than among countries, which should help to explain and rationalize the continued existence of trade linkages that are much tighter within than among countries. International migration might lessen these effects, either by increasing the strength of international linkages (depending on the strength of any remaining ties to the source country) or by lessening the cohesiveness of existing domestic networks. More systematic combination of migration and trade data is needed to test these possibilities. As for the border effects for migration, they need more systematic treatment with a larger sample of countries, since census data are likely to permit equations of the sort estimated here for Canada and the United States to be estimated for a much larger sample of countries, and to consider a greater number of international sources of migration for each of the receiving countries.

16. See Borjas (1995a).

Chapter 6

Borders and Growth

THIS CHAPTER has three sections. The first is a survey of several key approaches to the study of comparative growth. In the second section, growth-enhancing factors are surveyed, with consideration of the extent to which they are likely to be affected by national boundaries. The third section compares the growth results for national and regional economies, and then summarizes the possible implications of national boundaries for economic growth.

Alternative Approaches to Comparative Growth

Empirical study of comparative growth, initially based mainly on the data for industrial countries, preceded the renewed focus on formal growth theory. Fagerberg surveys much of the early empirical work on comparative growth, and reports the characteristic finding that international differences in per capita income levels and growth rates are due more to differences in the nature and efficiency of use of technology than to differing amounts of capital and labor.[1]

Convergence as Technological Catchup

Many studies showed convergence in the rates of growth of per capita incomes and rates of productivity growth among industrial countries in the years since 1950.[2]

1. See Fagerberg (1994).
2. See, e.g., Abramovitz (1979, 1986); Baumol (1986); Dowrick and Nguyen (1989); Dowrick and Gemmell (1991); Helliwell and Chung (1991a); Helliwell, Sturm, and Salou

Four important features are either explicit or implicit in these studies. First, technologies are to a significant extent nation-specific rather than freely available to all.[3] Second, the faster productivity growth of the initially poorer countries implies some international transfer of knowledge while closing the technology gap. Third, nations differ in the extent to which they have been able to close the technology gap. The degree to which a nation posses-ses institutions and contacts facilitating technological convergence can indicate whether it is expected to be qualified to join the "convergence club" of fast-growing countries.[4] This notion of convergence clubs becomes much more important when consider-ing global samples of countries, where there is substantial evidence of divergence and clustering.[5] Fourth, all studies start from a point where there is an established gap between a technological leader and the rest, with the causes of the original leap forward to be studied separately. These features imply considerable importance for national borders and national institutions. Researchers finding and explaining closure of technology gaps tend to attach substan-tial importance to national differences in institutions and networks in explaining how and why transferring technologies from one na-tional setting to another may be expensive and time-consuming.[6]

The technology gap literature also illustrates the importance of national border effects by showing that international differences in labor productivity are pervasive across all manufacturing in-dustries. Dollar, Wolff, and Baumol showed that international labor productivity gaps among thirteen industrial countries in 1980 were at least as great at the two-digit level of disaggregation as for manufacturing as a whole, while Dollar and Wolff showed that productivity convergence held over the 1963–82 period at the disaggregated level, although less strongly than for manufacturing as a whole.[7] The fact that convergence was stronger for the total

---

(1985); Maddison (1982). See also the comment by De Long (1988) and the reply by Baumol and Wolff (1988).

3. As revealed first in the pioneering study by Arrow and others (1961).

4. See Baumol (1986).

5. See Baumol and Wolff (1988); Quah (1996).

6. As noted by Fagerberg (1994).

7. See Dollar and Wolff (1988); Dollar, Wolff, and Baumol (1987).

than for the typical components shows that part, but only a small part, of the aggregate convergence was due to changes in industry mix, favoring industries with the fastest rates of technological convergence.

From the point of view of border effects, the most important feature of these results is the pervasiveness of international differences in productivity levels among the component industries of manufacturing, thus showing convincingly that similar technologies were not being applied even among the relatively open and (roughly) equally rich industrial countries. To make this point even more convincing as a demonstration of national border effects, it would be useful to have more studies comparing industry-level productivity differences across states or provinces within a single country to the corresponding differences among countries.[8]

The Classical Approach to Convergence Analysis

A related strand of research also used the enlarged range of countries covered by reasonably comparable data for gross domestic product (GDP) per capita at purchasing power parities to rekindle interest in the applicability of a fairly simple version of the neoclassical growth model in the form best known through the work of Robert Solow.[9] Several papers showed that making some allowance for accumulation of human as well as physical capital permitted a neoclassical model with constant returns to scale to explain a substantial fraction of global cross-national growth differences.[10] Two useful distinctions were drawn, one between conditional and unconditional convergence, and the other between convergence in growth rates and convergence in levels. Unconditional convergence is marked by convergence of growth rates or levels, which is evident in the raw data. Conditional convergence is represented by a significant negative partial effect of initial income levels in a multivariate explanation of comparative growth. The

8. Bernard and Jones (1996) find substantial differences across U.S. states in productivity levels in some but not all industries.

9. See Solow (1956); Summers and Heston (1991).

10. See, for example, Barro (1991); Barro and Sala-i-Martin (1995); Mankiw, Romer, and Weil (1992).

distinction between convergence of levels and of growth rates has always been crucial, but only became operational with the availability of purchasing power parity data, which permit international comparisons of levels of real per capita GDPs. By adjusting for international differences in the rates of growth of physical capital (measured by gross investment rates) and human capital (approximated by measures of schooling), Barro and Mankiw and others found significant evidence of conditional convergence of rates of growth of GDP per capita, using global samples including many developing countries. Mankiw et al. also showed significant evidence of longer-run differences in the levels of GDP per capita, even after allowing for differences in the stocks of physical and human capital.[11]

These studies were considered by their authors to provide evidence favoring the assumptions of the simple neoclassical model of economic growth, with all countries faced with the same production possibilities and possessing the same ability to harness them efficiently, provided they possessed the same levels of physical and human capital. These assumptions imply that international borders are irrelevant to the determination of efficiency levels. There was, however, already in hand the evidence described earlier showing substantial international differences in levels and rates of growth of technological efficiency. In addition, other strands of growth theory were ready to challenge the simple neoclassical model on several fronts: the assumed constant returns to scale at the national level, the assumed international equality of available technologies, and finally the exogenous nature of technological progress.

Endogenous Technology with National Spillovers

Early influential papers in endogenous growth diverged from the classical approach in several key respects.[12] Technical progress was made endogenous and was modeled in a way that presupposed increasing returns to scale at the national level. National

11. See Barro (1991); Mankiw, Romer, and Weil (1992).
12. As exemplified by Lucas (1988); Romer (1986). See also Romer (1994).

borders were assigned important roles as barriers serving to reflect whatever spillovers were created by the accumulation of knowledge in the domestic economy. This increased role for national borders developed in part in reaction to the fact that capital was not flowing from the rich to the poor countries at the high rate suggested by the neoclassical model.[13] After all, if the same technology were equally available and equally efficient in all countries, the large labor forces and low capital/output ratios in the poorer countries should have made investment returns very high there. Lucas was willing to accept that capital mobility might be high, and assumed that there were increasing national returns to the level of human capital. Thus countries that had large stocks of knowledge and human capital would have not just higher average levels of income but also higher rates of growth, since residents of the domestic economy were assumed to have access to at least some of the knowledge created by others in the same economy. Although the data did show some signs of growing income gaps between rich and poor countries, there was little evidence that larger countries had faster growth rates than smaller ones. Romer presented some evidence that richer countries did not systematically grow more slowly than poor ones, and concluded that divergence was more likely than convergence.[14] However, as noted above, conditional convergence is found in most studies. In any event the Romer hypothesis of increasing returns at the national level requires that countries with large GDPs, not large GDPs per capita, should grow at a faster rate than the rest. But there has been no systematic evidence that large economies grow more quickly than small ones.[15] This suggests either that knowledge spillovers are modest in scope or that they manage to cross national boundaries.

13. See Lucas (1990).

14. See Romer (1986).

15. Some evidence of returns to scale at the national level was found by Backus, Kehoe, and Kehoe (1992) and Helliwell and Chung (1991b), but not enough to carry the weight of explaining the observed pattern of international differences in levels and rates of growth of either GDP per capita or total factor productivity.

Endogenous Technology with International Spillovers

Another influential strand of literature shared the view that technical progress was endogenous, but rejected the notion that national borders would effectively contain spillovers from the accumulation of knowledge.[16] Empirical studies have used evidence from Organization for Economic Cooperation and Development (OECD) countries to show that international spillovers from research and development (R&D) spending are even larger, in the aggregate, than are domestic effects.[17] This evidence is described in more detail later in the chapter.

Convergence Clubs

Empirical work on comparative growth has emphasized that for global samples of countries the latter half of the twentieth century has generally not been marked by unconditional convergence of income levels. There has been no general tendency for the poorest countries to catch up to the richer ones.[18] Proponents of the convergence hypothesis have concentrated instead on conditional convergence, with convergence depending on a variety of factors. The fact that conditional convergence then shows up in global samples must mean that on average the poorer countries have lower scores on the various factors that tend to encourage growth. Some critics of the simpler forms of the convergence hypothesis have stressed instead the notion of convergence clubs, where the emphasis is on characterizing groups of countries whose growth paths and hence income levels share the same properties as those of other members of the same club.[19] In Baumol's earlier use of the term, there was a single "convergence club," and the trick was to find out how to join. In the more recent theoretical and empirical

16. See Grossman and Helpman (1993).

17. See Coe and Helpman (1995); Eaton and Kortum (1996).

18. However, Dowrick and Quiggin (1997) argue that the study of convergence using GDP data based on fixed-weight price indexes (as is the case with the data used in most convergence studies) is likely to understate the degree of income convergence of the poorer countries if the prices of richer countries are used to value GDP.

19. See Quah (1996); Galor (1996); Bernard and Durlauf (1996).

work on convergence clubs, there are likely to be two or more clubs, with the criteria for membership still not settled. As noted by Galor, the emphasis on convergence clubs, which can easily support the twin-peaked income distributions found in the work of Quah, reflects an extension of the convergence hypothesis to classify more systematically countries that share sufficient common features to place them in the same club.[20]

Research has not yet gone far enough to determine fully what sorts of common economic structures or policies place different countries in the same growth club. To some extent, the recent emphasis on the need to define the conditions necessary to encourage growth, or, conversely, the attempt to define the features of the low-growth countries, represents a return to much earlier work in the field of economic development, with its emphasis on the search for structural characteristics and policies enabling countries to "take off" into sustained growth.[21] Some growth clubs—for example, the eight high-performing East Asian economies whose growth performance was dubbed an "Asian Miracle" by the World Bank[22]—have been defined ex post facto, with attempts then made to see what may have been the secrets of their success.[23] Alternatively, some researchers use statistical methods to try to divide nations into groupings with common poles of convergence, leaving to later investigation the task of showing whether nations that share similar endpoints for their growth trajectories also share common geography, institutions, and resources.[24]

Factors Enhancing Growth

A varied body of empirical studies recognized that international convergence was taking place in rates of growth of income per capita, at least among some countries and over certain periods.

---

20. See Galor (1996); Quah (1996).
21. For example, Ohkawa and Rosovsky's (1973) concept of "social capability," also emphasized by Abramovitz (1990). The phrase "take off" is attributable to Rostow (1971).
22. See World Bank (1993).
23. For example, Rodrik (1994a, 1994b); Taylor (1995); Young (1992, 1995).
24. For example, Quah (1996); Durlauf and Johnson (1995).

This spurred a search for domestic factors and external linkages that could determine which countries were likely to join the convergence club and which were not. There follows a partial list of factors identified in the literature.

Openness and Growth

Evidence linking openness and growth could have important implications for any evaluation of the costs and benefits of border effects influencing movement of goods, capital, and population. That there should be a linkage between openness and growth follows naturally from the technological catchup models, since it would be surprising if all nations were equally able to absorb experience from abroad, and even more surprising if the fast-converging countries did not have a significant degree of openness to the rest of the world. How best to measure openness and to model its effects on growth are not immediately apparent, especially as researchers usually do not start with a strong presumption about which types of international linkage are likely to be most important in facilitating growth.

There have been two main approaches to studying the effects of openness and growth. One has been to measure different aspects of a country's openness and then to see whether they significantly alter the speed of conditional convergence. The second has been to define some criteria to divide countries into two clubs, one open and the other closed, and to see if the subsequent growth experiences of the two clubs are different. The first type of study has generally tended to show that a variety of openness variables, when added to cross-sectional growth equations, lead to faster growth. However, results from these studies have been neither uniform nor very robust to the choice of time period or measures used for openness.[25] More recent research with global samples has tended, with increasing regularity, to show a positive relationship.[26] An

25. Harrison (1996) surveyed the literature and tested a number of different specifications for several country samples, concluding that the weight of evidence favored a positive effect. However, Levine and Renelt (1992) and Levine and Zervos (1993) found such effects to be sometimes insignificant or unstable from one sample to the next.

26. See Ben-David (1993, 1994, 1996); Dollar (1992); Edwards (1993a, 1993b, 1997); Lee (1993).

important feature of the more recent literature is that measures of trade barriers, as reflected by tariffs and nontariff barriers, and the size of the black market premium on the exchange rate, tend to have more systematic effects on growth than do measures of trade intensity. This suggests that the ability to access foreign markets and ideas may be more important in determining a country's technological convergence than the actual volume of trade.

Evidence from selected groups of countries also supports the general conclusion that policy openness tends to be associated with faster subsequent growth. Among OECD countries, those with higher trade shares had faster rates of growth of technical progress, and hence faster convergence toward the attainment of best-practice efficiency levels.[27] Links between growth and policy openness were found to be tighter for the Asian economies, whether the measure of openness used was average tariff rates, the coverage of nontariff barriers, or the size of the black market premium. These measures of trade barriers were all higher for the South Asian than for the East and Southeast Asian countries, while the latter countries were in general faster growing.[28]

The second type of study of openness used some tests to divide countries into groups characterized as open or closed with respect to some set of policies or institutions. Ben-David used the joining of a trade bloc as a dividing line,[29] while Sachs and Warner used several measures of policies and institutions to define a set of open countries.[30] The Sachs and Warner results are very striking and are widely quoted. They found that subsequent growth rates were far higher for open than for closed economies. They also found strong unconditional convergence among the countries in their group of open economies, but no evidence of convergence in the closed group. They defined an open economy as one that achieved a

27. See Helliwell (1994c). This result did not depend on whether the measure of trade openness was adjusted for country size in the way suggested by Leamer (1988), since country size was already in the equation to capture possible national economies of scale.

28. The results are reported in Helliwell (1994a, 1995). The openness measures used were drawn from data published by the World Bank in conjunction with the *1991 World Development Report*.

29. See Ben-David (1993).

30. See Sachs and Warner (1995).

minimum threshold level of openness for each of several measures. Their threshold levels were not particularly high—for example, a black market exchange rate premium of less than 20 percent, and nontariff barriers covering less than 40 percent of imports—but the fact that several different tests had to be passed required an institutional structure and policy climate facilitating access to international ideas, even if the resulting levels of trade flows were nonetheless subject to substantial continuing restrictions.

Linkages between migration and growth have been studied less fully than have those between trade policy and growth. It has been argued that migration among the U.S. states has played an important role in the century-long convergence of per capita incomes among states following 1870.[31] Similarly, Taylor and Williamson emphasize the role of migration as a key factor in international convergence during the mass migrations at the end of the last century.[32] Studies of patent citations and of international collaborative research have also found that migration and scholarly exchanges play an important role in fostering international creation and transfer of new technologies. As noted in chapter 5, several studies show that international migrations tend to generate trade flows in their wake. The resulting consequences for growth and technological transfer have not been studied in a parallel way.

Education

All researchers have expected to find a robust relationship between education and economic growth. This is because almost any theory of growth offers a linkage between the accumulation of human capital and at least the level, and possibly the rate of growth, of potential output. Any model that permits capital accumulation to have beneficial spillovers can apply as well, or better, to the accumulation of knowledge than to the accumulation of bricks, mortar, and machines. Even without such spillovers, higher enrollment rates or increases in average levels of education are analogous to high rates of investment in physical capital, and

31. See Barro and Sala-i-Martin (1995).
32. See Taylor and Williamson (1994).

are expected to lead to higher rates of growth of output per capita. In theories of technological convergence, the level of education is often thought to play a role in facilitating the international transfer of ideas—a blueprint needs to be read with skill and care if it is to be correctly chosen and efficiently transferred. Lichtenberg and van Pottelsberghe de la Potterie found that countries with greater levels of outbound foreign direct investment could more effectively find and use foreign R&D.[33] It seems likely that such efforts to seek and acquire foreign R&D would be enhanced by higher levels of education, at least among certain key groups.

In the light of the breadth and unanimity of theoretical expectations, the empirical results linking education to aggregate growth have been rather scant. Barro and Lee carefully developed a large and varied database on internationally comparable measures of educational efforts and attainments.[34] They found strikingly little evidence of positive linkages between these measures and subsequent international differences in growth rates. Most global studies include some measure of educational effort or attainment to adjust for human capital accumulation, in the manner suggested by Mankiw and others,[35] but the results are often not robust to changes in the time period or the measure of education.[36]

Thus the jury is still out on the size of the effect that education plays in explaining comparative growth differences. Perhaps families, communities, educational institutions, and on-the-job training play such important and varying roles in education that conventionally measured differences in educational efforts and achievements do not adequately measure how education matters for growth. The evidence linking education and growth is generally positive, but neither pervasive nor tightly estimated. Since almost any theory of growth suggests that a strong education effect on growth should exist, the finding of a clearer relationship remains high on research agendas.

33. See Lichtenberg and van Pottelsberghe de la Potterie (1996).

34. See Barro and Lee (1993).

35. See Mankiw, Romer, and Weil (1992).

36. The same is true in more restricted samples. For example, differences in average growth rates among the Asian countries were not explained at all by differences among them in the measure of secondary school enrollment used by Mankiw, Romer, and Weil (Helliwell 1995).

Since the growing research on the economics of education continues to show high rates of return,[37] presumably the linkages to growth are there waiting to be exposed in due course.

Research and Development

If the empirical linkage between education and growth is weaker than other research suggests it should be, recent research on the role of industrial R&D may suffer from the reverse problem. There is a large and well-developed literature on the domestic linkages between R&D and the profitability and growth of firms. This research continues to show a variety of rates of return, generally high enough to support current levels of investment, but not out of the range of more generally attainable business investment returns. Recent research on the international and domestic growth spillovers from domestic R&D shows significant growth effects.[38]

A puzzling feature of the results is that they show spillovers and own-returns so large as to make R&D an almost impossibly attractive investment.[39] The total returns to R&D range upwards of 100 percent per annum, with most of the total return flowing from international spillovers. The research is naturally not able to assess the extent to which these spillovers are covered by payments for patents and licences. However, the estimated spillovers are so large compared to any data for actual payments as to guarantee that most of the estimated international growth effects are not the result of research findings being purchased and transferred abroad. This provides a partial resolution of the puzzle—that a

37. See Psacharopoulos (1985).

38. Eaton and Kortum (1996) find strong growth effects of both domestic and international R&D patenting for the OECD countries. Coe and Helpman (1995) find strong domestic and international growth effects from aggregate R&D spending in the same group of countries, while Coe, Helpman, and Hoffmaister (1997) find that there are also large spillover benefits to the developing countries. Bayoumi, Coe, and Helpman (1998) show the direct and indirect consequences of R&D spillovers to both OECD and developing countries. Bernstein and Yan (1997) estimate bilateral spillovers between Canadian and Japanese R&D.

39. To some extent this is reminiscent of previous research showing very high rates of return to infrastructure investment, while detailed cost-benefit analysis of the underlying projects did not show them exceeding a hurdle rate of return based on the government's cost of capital. Relevant studies are surveyed in Mintz and Preston (1994).

large part of the total return must represent external benefits not captured by those doing R&D.

Another partial answer to the puzzle is that domestic R&D may provide a better measure than does conventional educational attainment of a nation's capacity to obtain and make good use of foreign technologies. Hence some of what is estimated as a very high rate of return to R&D may reflect the fact that R&D is a good proxy for the kinds of skills, and the required degree of accessibility to foreign literature, universities, and laboratories, that most facilitate convergence. To the extent that this is true, then as convergence proceeds, measured spillovers will decrease. However, it should be noted that the high estimated spillovers are among the OECD countries themselves, many of which are close to ending their convergence process, and the spillovers do not seem to depend entirely on the R&D capacity of the receiving country. In addition, even if the remaining potential for convergence is included in the equation,[40] there is little reduction in the estimated spillovers from R&D. Further investigation may help to reveal how the high estimated returns are most appropriately divided among persistent external effects, high returns to the R&D investors, and growth more appropriately attributable to education or catchup. There is also the possibility that the strong relationship between R&D and growth may to some extent reflect a process in which the influence runs in the other direction, with high profits from past growth leading to high subsequent spending on R&D.

Despite uncertainty about the current size of the estimated domestic and international returns to R&D investment, it is interesting to use the available estimates to calculate R&D border effects analogous to those already calculated for goods, services, and population. Table 6.1 uses the results from Coe and Helpman as a basis for estimates of border effects for R&D spillovers.[41] The numbers relate to the domestic and international GDP effects of

<hr/>

40. As in Coe, Helpman, and Hoffmaister (1997).

41. See Coe and Helpman (1995). Border effects based on the results of Lichtenberg and van Pottelsberghe de la Potterie (1996) are even higher. Bayoumi, Coe, and Helpman (1998) have re-estimated their effects adopting the Lichtenberg and van Pottelsberghe de la Potterie (1996) suggestion for defining the foreign R&D capital stock series, and find results very similar to those used in table 6-1.

Table 6-1. *Border Estimates for Productivity Effects of R&D Spending*

	United States	Japan	Germany	France	Italy	United Kingdom	Canada
United States	1	3	10	19	21	14	3
Japan	37	1	197	347	418	445	281
Germany	30	35	1	19	26	33	208
France	57	107	23	1	38	61	632
Italy	207	485	53	77	1	234	1,575
United Kingdom	31	59	21	39	61	1	164
Canada	109	1,024	2,629	4,326	3,474	2,221	1

Notes: Border effects are based on elasticities found in table 5 of Coe and Helpman (1995, p. 873), which in turn are based on equation iii in tables 3 and A.7 of Coe and Helpman (1995, pp. 869, 883). Estimated border effect between importing (row) country and exporting (column) country is as follows: Border effect$_{rc}$ = Domestic elasticity (0.2339) × domestic R&D$_c$ / (C&H elasticity$_{rc}$ × domestic R&D$_r$).

R&D spending in the Group of Seven industrial countries, showing in each case the ratio of the net growth effects from a dollar of domestic R&D compared to the return to the domestic economy from the same dollar being spent in the country on the other side of the border.[42] Two border effects are shown for each pair of countries, one relating to inbound and the other to outbound R&D effects. The rows show the country doing the R&D, while the columns show the countries for which the border effects are being calculated. For example, the number 53 in the Italy row and the Germany column shows the ratio of the GDP effects in Germany of German R&D compared to Italian R&D. If there were no border effects, and if distance did not matter either, then we would expect the numbers to be close to 1.0, showing that the effects of R&D on German GDP did not depend on whether the R&D was done in Germany or in another country. The border effects for R&D are much larger than those found earlier for merchandise trade.

42. There is a possibility that these border effects may be overestimates of the true border effects if the private domestic returns to R&D are not being properly accounted for in the measures of capital stock used in the calculation of the measures of technical progress. The productivity growth rates used by Coe and Helpman as their dependent variables are based on GDP growth minus weighted averages of the growth rates of labor and capital inputs. The capital stocks used do not include the stocks of R&D, so that countries with unusually high R&D spending may have estimates of domestic spillovers that are exaggerated by the inclusion of some of the normal private return to R&D.

There are many reasons why one might expect the productivity growth effects of R&D spending to be higher in the country in which the R&D is undertaken. Two purely measurement issues tend to make the R&D border effects higher than those already reported for merchandise trade. One is that distance is not included in the estimated models, and there may be "transportation costs" for knowledge analogous to those for merchandise trade. The analogy is rough, of course, as there are identifiable costs of moving goods from one location to another, and these are absent or negligible in the case of knowledge. However, one of the implications of the argument, consistent with evidence in this book, is that the effects of distance relate to much more than the costs of moving merchandise. Movements of both merchandise and knowledge are likely to be less active where there are fewer personal and institutional linkages, and less knowledge of the opportunities and risks of new commercial ventures. Given the fact that geographic closeness provides automatic familiarity with many aspects of the society in which one is living, it is to be expected that commercial as well as social contacts will start close to home and extend farther only as reliable knowledge of better opportunities further afield comes to dominate the status quo.[43] This is why it was important to evaluate border effects for merchandise trade in the context of a gravity model taking account of distance. Otherwise, there might be a risk of ascribing to border effects something that was more correctly ascribed to distance.

The argument of this book is that the reductions in reliable information take place as distance increases and as national borders are crossed, because social and knowledge networks that fuel personal and economic transactions are more dense within national borders and become less dense as distance increases. Thus we might expect to find R&D border effects to be larger than those for trade, since there is no direct allowance for distance in the calculations shown in table 6-1.[44] It is possible to estimate the likely size

---

43. See Almeida and Kogut (1998).
44. This is because the stocks of domestic and foreign R&D are both entered directly in the Coe and Helpman estimation. The effects of distance differences among the foreign

of this bias by re-estimating the merchandise trade border effects excluding the distance variable, to provide something that is more conceptually akin to the R&D border effects shown in table 6-1. If distance is left out of the simplest trade equation using the global data sample of chapter 3, the OECD border coefficient rises from 2.39 to 5.45, implying an increase in the border effect from 10.9 to 233. This substantially narrows the difference between the estimated border effects for R&D and for merchandise trade.[45]

The second measurement reason for the high border effects in table 6-1 is that the productivity growth rates used by Coe and Helpman are net of the output growth contributions of labor and physical capital, but not of the increases in the stocks of domestic (or foreign) R&D. Thus any R&D capital-deepening effect, to the extent that it differs for domestic and foreign users of the results of the R&D, is left to be explained as part of the domestic return to domestic R&D.

In addition to the measurement issues, there are more general reasons why border effects for R&D might differ from those for merchandise trade. To the extent that there are local and national differences in tastes, natural resources, human resources, and current industrial structures, local problems would be expected to be the primary focus of R&D investment. To the extent that R&D is aimed at solving particularly local problems, it should not be expected to offer equivalent advantage to communities with different structures and problems. On the other hand, many of the tariff and nontariff barriers that apply to merchandise trade do not apply to transfers of knowledge. The availability of knowledge to those outside the group doing the R&D is limited chiefly by ownership of patents and the confidentiality with which the knowledge is handled. These restrictions on availability usually apply equally to all those outside the commercial ambit of the firm doing the R&D, without special attention to national boundaries.

---

sources of R&D spillovers are implicitly allowed for, as both sets of authors weight the stocks of foreign R&D by the use of bilateral imports, which the gravity models show to be smaller for trading pairs separated by larger distances.

45. It also suggests the possible importance of considering distance more explicitly in models of R&D spillovers. Perhaps the distance effect implied by using trade flows to weight the effects of foreign R&D is correct, but alternatives should at least be considered.

There are exceptions to this, of course, as national boundaries are sometimes used to define technology-sharing groups, and defense or national security grounds are used to justify restrictions on international transfers of some advanced technologies. But there is no strong reason to suppose that the use of national boundaries to define information-sharing groups should be significantly greater than for trade in goods and services. There may be some linkages between international knowledge transfers and migration. Studies have shown increasing intensity of cross-border research and citations. Such trends may be harbingers for declining future border effects for R&D, since international collaborations are more likely to give rise to knowledge which is equally available from the outset in several countries.

Whatever may be the results of future trends, the results shown in table 6-1 suggest that current border effects for R&D are very large. This may be in part due to measurement issues, and may be expected to change as research continues. Being based on information quite different from that employed in the estimation of border effects for trade, prices, and capital movements, the R&D border effects tend to add to the general strength of the conclusion that national boundaries are strongly significant in defining the scope of contacts, contracts, and institutions that govern the density of economic, social, and information networks.

Income Equality, Macroeconomic Stability, and Growth

Some studies suggest that countries with greater equality of income distribution also have higher average growth rates. In these papers, the primary reason offered is that democracies with more equal distributions of income are more likely to have median voters that are willing to support macroeconomic stabilization and tax regimes that favor growth.[46] There is also more direct evidence that macroeconomic stability, especially as measured by low infla-

---

46. See Alesina and Rodrik (1994); Persson and Tabellini (1994). Knack and Keefer (1997b) show that the link between inequality and growth applies even for nondemocracies, suggesting that the link is more general than is implied by the median voter model.

tion rates, encourages faster growth, with the exact channels not made explicit.[47]

Inequality, Trade, and Growth

One central economic puzzle in developed countries in the 1980s and 1990s has been the increased polarization of income and employment prospects. In the United States, the polarization occurred mainly in wages and incomes. Higher unemployment rates polarized incomes in continental Europe, while some combination of the two sources was evident in the United Kingdom and Canada. Two of the main candidates have been trade- and skill-biased technical progress. Trade explanations are based on the idea that the increasing availability of products embodying low-cost labor in poor countries has decreased the demand for low-skilled workers in the richer industrial countries. The skill-biased technology explanation assumes that newer technologies need higher average skill levels and have twisted the mix of labor demand in favor of the higher-skilled.

The debate about the relative importance of these two lines of explanation is still in midcourse. Most attempts to balance the scales attach some importance to both factors. Trade flows are regarded as being too small to have had such large effects on employment and income distribution, but most analysts still give the trade argument some weight. Skill-biased technological change seems too much of a black box to be quickly accepted. It has been gaining credence, at least relative to the trade-only hypothesis, because similar patterns of increased skill premiums have been occurring even in much poorer countries.

How are these issues related to the study of border effects? To the extent that trade is the source of increased income inequality, and if increased inequality eventually leads to growth-reducing policies, then the increased openness of developing countries may be exacting a growth penalty not yet evident. On the other hand, the current size of border effects seems to support the argument that observed changes in trade prices and volumes could not be

47. See Bruno (1993); Fischer (1993); Gylfason (1991).

the cause of such pervasive changes in the domestic income distribution. This point appears even stronger in the light of evidence that the changes in the distribution of incomes between high- and lower-skilled workers pervade all industries, without special concentration in the industries most vulnerable to direct competition from imported products.

Institutions and Growth

The need to explain the great variety of growth performance among developing countries has encouraged increased emphasis on describing the structure and quality of institutions whose performance may be considered important to the achievement of growth. The candidates have included legal, market, social, and political institutions. Some of this interest has been long-standing, as exemplified by the extensive literature on the linkages between democracy and growth.[48] More recently, especially in the attempt to understand the depth and length of the drops in output and incomes in the Eastern European countries in the 1990s, more attention has been paid to legal, market, and social institutions. Some studies emphasize the importance of relatively unfettered investment and business activities, while others stress the necessity for a legal system that establishes a framework of enforceable rules and restraints on the operation of both market and nonmarket activities.[49] Still others have noted the breakdown of both social trust and social safety nets, and have found some evidence that shared values and norms are conducive to higher levels of economic performance.

The Role of National Borders

This section first examines the links between regional and national convergence. It then asks whether home preferences hamper

48. See Sirowy and Inkeles (1990) and Helliwell (1994b) for surveys and references to this literature.
49. See Knack and Keefer (1995); Mauro (1995).

growth, thereby introducing the more general discussion in chapter 7.

Regional and National Convergence Compared

One of the empirical puzzles that needs to be dealt with is the apparent finding that conditional convergence of growth rates has been taking place at roughly comparable rates among states in the United States, among provinces in Canada, among subnational regions in several European countries, and among nation-states.[50] If national borders are as important as the evidence in previous chapters would indicate, then it seems puzzling that the convergence process should be so similar. One possible interpretation is that this result is largely coincidental, with the causes of initial divergence and the factors determining the rates of subsequent convergence differing within and among countries. Under this interpretation, standardization for all other influences would show that national transmission of whatever fuels convergence would turn out to be faster than international transmission. This interpretation is supported by a variety of cross-national studies finding that countries that are more open also converge faster. Conversely, closed countries do not converge at all.[51]

Another interpretation of the puzzle might be that the degree of openness required to achieve and maintain convergence is much smaller than that entailed by the density of economic exchanges within a national economy. If there is some critical degree of openness required to achieve knowledge transfers of the sort required to achieve convergence, as the binary categorization proposed by Sachs and Warner seems to suggest, then further integration beyond that may not be important for growth. This would be consistent with an interpretation I offered earlier to explain how big and small economies could have such similar levels of GDP per capita in the face of such big border effects on trade densities. The possibility was raised that if additional trade mainly increases the variety of largely similar goods, there might be

50. See Barro and Sala-i-Martin (1995); Sala-i-Martin (1996a, 1996b).
51. See Ben-David and Rahman (1996); Sachs and Warner (1995).

little gain of welfare if the variety were further increased. (A difficulty here may be that the national income data used to compare incomes per capita may not take adequate account of the influence of product variety on consumer utility.)

Do Home Preferences Hamper Growth?

Assessing the possible growth implications of home preferences is not a job for a one-handed economist, nor for the faint of heart. There are just too many possibilities and too many factors changing underfoot. One straightforward conclusion that could be made from confronting the strong border effects documented in this book with the evidence linking openness and growth is that these border effects cause growth to be lower than it otherwise would be. After all, if more open countries grow faster, then would it not be better for growth if there were no border effects at all? Seen in this context, globalization is good for growth, and the faster the better. However, the evidence on openness and growth relates chiefly to the establishment of the necessary conditions for technological convergence to take place, and does not speak directly to the question of how much openness is needed. Research has so far not been able to pinpoint which are the crucial aspects of openness. Do they relate chiefly to avenues for goods trade, for direct or portfolio investment flows, for transnational education, to more open access to ideas, or to harmonized standards for products, legal systems, contracts, and trading rules? It also remains to establish how much homogenization is required and where diminishing returns may be setting in.

By most measures, global linkages have been growing over the past five decades, and there has indeed been substantial convergence among at least the industrialized countries. Yet over the last quarter century, since the middle of the 1970s, real GDP growth on average in the industrial countries has been substantially slower than over the preceding twenty-five years. To some extent this is a necessary consequence of the convergence process, for ever-narrower technology gaps imply ever-smaller gains from further convergence. Growth since 1973 has slowed for both leaders and followers. Thus the slowdown must represent more than just diminution of the size of the remaining technology gap. Furthermore, if still greater openness is good for growth, it should affect the growth possibilities for the richer as well as the catching-up countries, and should provide increasing growth possibilities for all. The facts that growth in living standards among the richest countries has stagnated over the last quarter of the twentieth century, and that there have been associated increases in income inequality, due in varying degrees to rising unemployment and greater wage dispersion, suggest, as argued by some of the literature on trade and growth, that to some extent the recent convergence may involve losers as well as gainers.

A two-handed interpretation of the evidence would recognize the possible gains from further increases in the international flows of goods, services, people, and ideas, while acknowledging also the likelihood that decreasing returns to additional trade and investment may be setting in. What may be most important for convergence may be sufficient openness for ideas and trade to move freely both within and between countries. If, in these circumstances, home preferences continue to be important, this may reflect an equilibrium in which the lower costs of operating within a context of known norms and institutions are enough to offset any growth gains from further increases in the density of international linkages.

Chapter 7

How Do Border Effects Matter?

T HE PREVIOUS chapters have attempted to measure the importance of national boundaries as determinants of current levels
and patterns of trade, investment, migration, and growth. This
concluding chapter summarizes the evidence and assesses its implications for economic theory and policy.

Some attempts are also made to produce a scorecard of good
and bad features of the continuing cohesion of national economies. It
is one thing to measure the relative densities of economic activity
within and between nations, and the results on this score should be
fairly convincing. It is more difficult to evaluate the economic and
social causes and consequences of these differences. The issues
should at least be posed.

This chapter does so in stages. First there is a summary of the
levels and trends in border effects. Then there is some discussion of their implications for international trade theory and
policy, followed by a consideration of some of the reasons for
thinking that border effects might have both good and bad
consequences. The final section attempts to balance the good
and bad consequences of border effects to see if some beneficial
equilibrium is possible in which border effects are high enough to
serve useful sorting and identifying functions while being low
enough to permit productive flows of trade and information to be
easily realized.

Levels and Trends in Border Effects

There appear to be two main factors explaining changes in border effects for merchandise trade: the reduction of formal trade barriers, as exemplified by the European Union (EU) and the Canada–United States Free Trade Agreement (FTA), and changes in the level of a country's per capita income. No apparent trend, over the 1988–92 period, was found in the border effects for trade among the Organization for Economic Cooperation and Development (OECD) countries, although the levels of border effects are smaller for trade among EU members and between countries sharing a common language. The border effects for trade among countries in the global sample show some signs of decline over the 1988–92 period, mainly traceable to increases in their average per capita incomes, but also attributable to reductions in trade barriers. Merchandise border effects between Canada and the United States, based on the latest available data, were about 17 in 1988, fell to about 12 by 1993, and have remained at roughly the same level through 1996. It is too early to know if this represents full adjustment to the FTA, or whether there is more to come.

If the precedent of the U.S.–Canada 1965 Auto Pact is helpful, it suggests that the post-FTA adjustments may have largely run their course. After the Auto Pact came into force, trade in cars and parts grew from about 7 percent to more than 20 percent of total merchandise trade within 5 years.[1] Subsequent trends have been mainly downward in response to increases in the value of resource trade, the changing fortunes of the North American automotive industry, and increasing integration of other industries. The current share is about 11 percent. Although border effects were found to have been eliminated among the major car-producing states and provinces, they remain high for other trading pairs. Border effects in most other industries are higher than those estimated using data for aggregate merchandise trade.

Estimates for service trade, based on aggregate data for interprovincial and Canada–U.S. trade in services, and working from

1. Bank of Canada (1969).

benchmark estimates for merchandise trade, show that inter-provincial trade in services is between thirty and forty times more intense than that between provinces and states.

Chapter 3 extended the study of border effects to merchandise trade flows among and within samples of OECD and developing countries. Domestic sales of goods were found to be about ten times greater than sales among OECD countries, in the absence of trade bloc and common language effects, both of which reduce the size of border effects. When the sample was increased to include domestic and international trade for eleven developing countries, the border effects were found to be even larger and subject to a downward trend over the 1988–92 sample period. Border effects were found to be up to 100 or more for some developing countries, but all the differences among countries were explained by a vari-able making the border effect depend on each country's per capita income. In 1992, average border effects for the large sample were about 20 for a country of average per capita income. In the absence of data for internal trade distances for most countries, these estimates of border effects for the international sample need to be treated with caution.

Results surveyed in chapter 4 show that the border effects for merchandise trade have counterparts in prices. It might be ex-pected that pressures to arbitrage away price differentials are less intense where actual and potential trade flows are smaller, as is the case at greater distances and across national boundaries. The Engel and Rogers results show that this is indeed the case, as consumer price covariability is much higher among Canadian cities than between Canadian and U.S. cities, while also being higher for domestic cities that are closer together.[2] These results are consistent with the results reported in chapter 2 for merchan-dise trade flows.

Chapter 4 also reports evidence showing that capital mobility is much greater within countries than from one country to another. This is shown by portfolio studies, which continually reveal very limited investments in foreign assets, as well as by studies of correlations between savings and investment rates. The marked

2. See Engel and Rogers (1996).

correlation between national savings and domestic investment rates has long been used as a measure of the immobility of capital across national borders. A new study reported in chapter 4 pools OECD country data with Canadian interprovincial data to show a high correlation of savings and investment rates across countries coupled with a zero correlation across provinces. This suggests that savings in one province are easily transferred to become real investment in other provinces, while the same is not true across national boundaries.

Chapter 5 uses census data to compare interprovincial and interstate migration with immigration from the other country, showing that after allowing for the effects of distance, population size, and income differentials, a resident of a Canadian province is almost one hundred times as likely to have been born in another province as to have been born in the United States. The border effects for southbound migration are much smaller, but still very significant. There is international evidence that migration flows tend to increase trade flows in their wake, partly through imported tastes but also reflecting transfer of knowledge about trade opportunities and business norms in the other country.

Chapter 6 reviews the linkages between borders and growth. The main empirical result relates to border effects for the spillovers from industrial research and development, which are estimated to be several times higher than those for merchandise trade. The second key result from the literature surveyed in chapter 6 is that growth is faster among developing countries that are sufficiently open to be able to import and make use of technologies already in use elsewhere in the world. This suggests that at least some degree of openness has a positive effect on growth. To make this result compatible with strong border effects and the fact that larger countries do not tend to grow faster, it was suggested that there might be a link in the relationship between openness and growth—that some degree of openness is required to achieve access to valuable foreign opportunities for trade and technological improvement, but that trade ties beyond some level of intensity might not contribute much to growth possibilities.

Overall, the evidence presented and surveyed in chapters 2–6 provides a consistent impression that national economies have internal economic linkages very much tighter than those between nations. Next it is necessary to assess the implications of these findings.

Implications for Trade Theory and Policy

The striking size and pervasiveness of border effects reveal that the global economy of the 1990s is really a patchwork of national economies, stitched together by threads of trade and investment that are much weaker than the economic fabric of nations. This makes untenable many of the central assumptions of international economics, and requires a major rethinking about how best to model international flows of goods and capital. For those who follow the empirical literature on international trade, this should not come as a complete surprise. Researchers have for many years been unable to verify the central empirical implications of international trade theory based on the Heckscher-Ohlin-Vanek (HOV) general equilibrium, full-information, global-technology model of the distribution of production and trade. The problem, as Trefler puts it, is that there is too much missing trade—countries do not trade as much with each other as their endowment differences would suggest they would under the assumptions of equal technologies, equal tastes, and fully informed perfect competition.[3] What is not clear from the failure of the trade model to explain international trade patterns is whether the required assumptions are ever sufficiently realistic for the model to help explain actual patterns of trade, or if international trade is just the wrong place to expect the model to work.

In the light of the very large border effects that have been spelled out in this book, one might expect that the HOV model would work better for trade within countries than for trade between them. An important recent paper by Davis and others shows just that.[4] When the trade model is set up on the standard assumptions, it fails to explain international trade, but does very well in explain-

3. See Trefler (1995).
4. See Davis and others (1997).

ing the distribution of production among Japanese prefectures. This leads naturally to the inference that the conditions for full economic integration are met to a far higher degree among regions within Japan than they are among nations, just as would be implied by strong national border effects.

One stark way of putting the case is that there is nothing wrong with international trade theory except its title. If "international" is taken out of the title the theory has much to contribute, even in its simpler versions, to the explanation of trade patterns of regions within a country. That may be good news for the basic theoretical structure, but would leave international trade theory rather short of underpinnings. Thus the search is on for simple ways of building in border effects of the most relevant sort, thereby developing a revised trade theory that does a reasonable job of explaining international as well as intranational trade flows. Davis and others find that in their data it is most important to drop the assumptions of internationally identical technologies and factor price equalization. Neither of these results should come as a surprise, given the chapter 4 evidence about the strong border effects for prices, and the chapter 6 survey of many studies showing large international differences in the levels and rates of growth of productivity. With those key adjustments made, Davis and others find little further empirical need to assume different tastes in different countries. Trefler, on the other hand, finds large improvements from assuming a combination of tastes favoring national products and technologies that differ internationally in their levels of technical progress.[5]

In part in response to the sharp growth in intraindustry trade flows, and in part in response to the empirical failures of trade models based solely on endowment differences, much trade theory of the past twenty years has departed from the perfectly competitive model to emphasize monopolistic competition in differentiated products. This literature can quite easily be extended to include border effects by assuming that products are differentiated

---

5. See Trefler (1995, pp. 1043–44). In another study that distinguishes goods by nation of origin, Bröcker (1997) uses a spatial, computable general equilibrium model, with parameters chosen to reflect European trade patterns, to estimate implied border effects, and finds them almost as high as those originally estimated by McCallum (1995).

also by their place of production. The problem with this approach to product characteristics is that it is increasingly difficult for consumers to know, and perhaps unlikely that they would care, which components came from which countries or even where the product was assembled.

There has also been a resurgence of interest in the geographic basis for trade and in the extent to which established trade patterns have continuity.[6] By emphasizing that distance matters, this literature ties in very well with the geographic basis of the gravity model used here to estimate border effects. Perhaps because it preceded the finding of strong border effects, the geographic trade literature emphasizes history and location, with an emphasis on local rather than national agglomerations and spillovers. The borders evidence suggests that geography and national borders have separate but analogous effects in setting patterns for economic activity, with history mattering in both cases.

There is much less concern within trade theory for the importance of institutions, particularly those embodying national differences of a sort that might create border effects. Since the prevalence of border effects is likely to spark interest in finding the pattern of causes, more attention seems likely to fall on a variety of institutional differences that might cause national economies to be internally tight. What are some of the likely candidates?

Much of the literature stressing the importance of institutions relates to units smaller than the nation-state. In dealing with the common features of families, friends, and firms, Ben-Porath argued that these and other institutions play a key role in establishing the identity of their participants, thereby reducing uncertainties that would otherwise hamper economic relations.[7] Although he emphasized the efficiency roles of families, friends, and firms, the same reasoning can be applied also to communities and nation-states. The usefulness of the identity established by the units, whether the family, the social group, or the nation, has two aspects: the rights, expectations, and responsibilities of members in their relations with one another, and the credibility of the family unit or

6. See Krugman (1991) for an outline of the main elements of geography-based trade.
7. See Ben-Porath (1980).

group in its dealings with others. Ben-Porath argues that groupings at different levels serve different purposes and are not mutually exclusive.[8] Family units are small and may involve high degrees of shared values and obligations; firms may have more purpose-specific structure and rules; and larger groupings may involve more loosely defined expectations about the rights and responsibilities of members toward each other and toward the rest of the world.

Industrial organization researchers have long sought for reasons why firms are useful institutions, and some of the reasons they have emphasized can be applied to some extent to the nation-state. Oliver Williamson has emphasized the importance of transaction costs, and argued that the existence and structure of firms can be best analyzed as means of reducing transaction costs. Firms and other long-term relationships among those involved in joint commercial activities are seen as "structures that facilitate gapfilling, dispute settlement, adaptation, and so on."[9] Williamson argues that the need for institutions to efficiently deal with unforeseen contingencies is especially great where investment involves large, irreversible commitments of effort and capital to specific purposes. He argues that the appropriate scale and nature of the firm are best understood in terms of their effects on transaction costs, rather than on the more usual analysis based on economies of scale in production. Much the same could be said of the nation-state—here the key issue is whether the grouping of such a high proportion of transactions within national markets is justified in terms of lower transaction costs provided by the ability to operate within commonly understood procedures and within trusted and well-understood channels of distribution.

Oliver Hart agrees that firms are useful in providing patterns of mutual dependence to deal efficiently with contingencies that cannot efficiently be made subject to contract.[10] He also analyzes the consequences of mergers between firms, emphasizing the

---

8. Johansson and Westin (1994) develop several models showing how different types of networks influence trade flows.

9. Williamson (1989, p. 139). A similar case was made previously by Alchian and Demsetz (1972).

10. See Hart (1995).

transfer of property rights that takes place when control changes. He argues that firms deal best with the problems of incomplete contracts if they assign powers and responsibilities so that individuals do their best for the enterprise. The long-term nature of these relationships serves to control what otherwise might be incentives for opportunistic behavior at the expense of others. He argues that firms provide more effective means for balancing powers and responsibilities than can be provided through contracts and the courts, although he also notes, as many others have done, that high levels of trust may be more effective than either firms or the courts.[11]

The argument has implications for the analysis of border effects. Given the greater ease of operating within known structures and networks, most firms themselves have denser structures within than among nations. Second, the existence of separate national institutions, cultures, and information networks lowers the uncertainty of operations within the national economies with which managers and shareholders are familiar. Thus the nation-state itself provides some of the same familiarity and mutual dependency that firms provide. It is a feature of the industrial organization literature, and of much of the institutional literature, that firms and other institutions break the anonymity of the market for good reason—to provide participants with enough confidence in others to be able to proceed even though the future is uncertain, commitments must be made, and contingencies cannot be fully hedged.

Although the different types of uncertainty-reducing groups are not mutually exclusive, they may to some extent be substitutes for one another. For instance, as the economic and institutional development proceeds in a society, more attention and importance are transferred from the family to the rules and expectations set by larger units. All of these units may improve the efficiency of economic exchange by using reciprocal long-term rights, expectations, and responsibilities to supplant the need for the expensive and complex contracts that would be required to support cooperation and exchange if the world were at once impersonal and uncertain. Different classes of institutions make exchange and

11. See Hart (1995, p. 1).

cooperation manageable by reducing uncertainty and by setting the approximate terms of reciprocity to be expected in economic relations within the group, and to a lesser extent between groups. Whether the nation-state is a superior or inferior source of these functions is not obvious. What is clearer is that as long as national institutions, populations, trust, and tastes differ as much as they do, the industrial organization and other institutional literatures would predict that transaction costs will remain much lower within than among national economies, even in the absence of any border taxes or regulations affecting the movements of goods and services.

Turning to trade and other policies, border effects have several implications. The nature of the implications turns to a large extent on beliefs about the sources, nature, and usefulness of border effects. It is quite common within economics to treat national borders as reflecting only the location for the imposition of taxes and other impediments to trade.[12] If this should turn out to be an appropriate conclusion, then one would expect to see continuing arguments in favor of reducing policy-based border barriers, and to see border effects vanishing soon after. Under this interpretation, if border effects did not vanish, even when there were no policies in place to maintain them, then it would be because the trading system has multiple equilibria of roughly equal value, with the previous patterns being maintained in the absence of sufficient reasons for change.

An alternative view, which may be hard to distinguish in practice, would be that border effects do serve economic purposes of the sorts already described. This would lessen the presumption that dismantling border-based policies would lead to large increases in trade and welfare, and would enhance the expectation that border effects will survive with or without policies that may have helped to create or maintain them.

---

12. For example, Krugman (1991, pp. 71–72) argues "Nations matter . . . because they have governments whose polices affect the movements of goods and factors. In particular, national boundaries often act as boundaries to trade and factor mobility. Every modern nation has restrictions on labor mobility. Many nations place restrictions on the movement of capital, or at least threaten to do so. And actual or potential limits on trade are pervasive, in spite of the best efforts of trade negotiators. . . . But in any case the point is that countries should be defined in terms of their restrictions."

Whether border effects are based in government policies or in private contacts and inclinations, or some complex combination, they have important implications for the design of monetary areas. Cesarano argues that the literature on optimal currency areas should start with border effects as a fact, and then consider the consequences for choices about currency areas.[13] He says that the case for national currencies is stronger than the literature would suggest, since border effects are more pervasive than is assumed either in the theory or in most policy discussions.

Are Border Effects Efficient?

Is there a case to be made for national borders? If so, it is likely to take the form, at least in part, of sharply diminishing returns to openness beyond some degree. The diminishing case for increased openness would then be coupled with a tendency for past patterns of trade and activity to be maintained in the absence of compelling incentives to change. It is worth asking if an additional case might be made in which borders play an economically useful role in sorting individuals, groups, institutions, and transactions in ways that increase the overall efficiency of economic outcomes. There could be two elements in such a case. One is the need for institutions that establish identities as means of assuring the structure and enforceability of long-term economic relations. Underlying this case, as described in the previous section, is the presumed usefulness of predictable institutions and behavior, coupled with some degree of shared values, including trust, to exist at the national level. The second element of the case, to be considered later, is the usefulness of some degree of economic distance to make investment opportunities tangible and exploitable by firms.

The first element, based on institutional differences, must rely on the likely continuity of international differences in the densities of a variety of familial, linguistic, cultural, social, and business networks, coupled with the presumption that these networks pro-

13. See Cesarano (1997).

vide efficient means of providing levels of trust sufficient to promote low-cost exchanges.[14]

Drivers from polite cities shake their heads in fear and wonder when they face the fast-paced streets of an aggressive driver's city. Drivers from cities where aggressive driving is the norm have their own wonder and exasperation when they travel to the land of patient queues. Whatever may be one's preferences in the abstract, it is probably true that driving in cities of either type is safer than in a city where there is no basis of expectations about how other drivers will react. Shared standards and norms reduce uncertainty and transaction costs.[15] If the shared norms include perceptions of mutual trustworthiness, they can also increase the rationality of assuming that others are to be trusted, which in turn increases the range and lowers the cost of mutually beneficial exchanges.[16]

Does globalization offer the promise of harmonized global standards and shared values, or does it threaten the stability of currently established community values without offering anything in their place? There are examples of both types. One of the unsung committees of the OECD has been working for many years on internationally standardized highway signage to make the

14. If these networks differ in efficiency, and can be relatively easily copied in another nation, then welfare may be increased by institutional homogenization, as illustrated by Casella's (1992) modeling of political integration. On the other hand, if institutional differences provide helpful means of reducing uncertainty and transaction costs, then they are likely to be efficient and enduring, as argued by Greif (1992).

15. The case for this is made by Coleman (1990), Knack and Keefer (1997a), and Platteau (1994), among others. The fact that predictability of driving behavior may be a good thing does not imply that all norms are of equal value. Ashok Kotwal tells me that New Delhi drivers all use their high beams, on the grounds that it is better to see as much as you can in the face of all the blinding lights, while drivers in Bombay and most other cities of the world use low beams.

16. It has been noted that trust and legal recourse may be to some extent substitutable, with trust being more necessary where legally enforceable contracts are not available, and vice versa. This notion is supported by the cross-national results of Knack and Keefer (1997a), showing a negative correlation between average levels of trust and the number of lawyers per capita. The argument that trust is a cheaper and more effective alternative for increasing the assuredness of contracts has a long history. For example, "Genovesi insisted [that]. . . . civil contracts . . . rely more heavily on trust than they do upon the possibility— always precarious—of enforcing them. . . . In the absence of trust, he pointed out, 'There can be no certainty in contracts and hence no force to the laws' and a society in that condition is effectively reduced 'to a state of semi-savagery.'" (1803, pp. 113–16; quoted in Pagden 1988, p. 136).

basic rules of the local roads understood by drivers from other countries. That may not help much in predicting the reactions of other drivers, but at least it shows some of the signals and constraints to which all drivers are expected to respond. On the other hand, Rodrik has argued that increased globalization increases the uncertainty and inequality of domestic incomes, and raises the demand for and costs of social assistance programs to help those most affected. At the same time, "The owners of internationally mobile factors become disengaged from their local communities and disinterested in their development and prosperity."[17]

As documented by studies over many years, national boundaries mark cleavages in social capital, as measured by differences in participation in voluntary organizations and in beliefs about the extent to which others can be trusted.[18] Putnam collected much evidence from Italian regions showing that higher levels of these measures of social capital are conducive to more widespread satisfaction with the efficiency of government, as well as evidence that regional governments in those regions are in fact more efficient.[19] There is also some evidence that regions or countries with higher levels of social capital also have higher rates of growth.[20] The reasons for this relate to the beneficial effects of trust as a cost-reducing lubricant for economic and social transactions.[21] As noted in chapter 5, migrants tend to bring norms and social capital with them. The effects on aggregate trust levels in the communities of origin and destination are less clear. There is some cross-national evidence that aggregate levels of trust and civic participation are lower in countries with higher levels of ethnic heterogeneity.[22] There is no direct evidence on whether there is any offsetting

17. See Rodrik (1997, p. 70).
18. Almond and Verba (1963) were among the first to systematically survey and report international differences in trust and participation, and some of their questions have remained at the center of subsequent research. The World Values Survey (Inglehart, Nevitte, and Basanez, 1996) has documented continuing international differences.
19. See Putnam (1993).
20. See Helliwell and Putnam (1995) for evidence on the Italian regions and Knack and Keefer (1997a) for evidence from a sample of twenty-nine national market economies.
21. For this argument in more detail, see, among others, Dasgupta (1988); Knack and Keefer (1997a); Platteau (1994); Putnam (1993).
22. See Knack and Keefer (1997a, table VII).

increase in the feelings of trust between the countries of origin and destination.

What is even less clear is the effect that globalization, whether driven by increasing trade, investment, migration, or information flows, is having on either national or global average levels of trust and participation. On the negative side, trade and global technologies are sharing much of the blame for increasing polarization of incomes and opportunities in many national economies, with well-documented strains on the social safety nets and probably on the sense of social cohesion as well. Putting aside these strains, what can be said about shared values and institutions in the global village? Is the village analogy apt? Are there some limits to the extent of the community with which individuals can share enough fellow feeling to have a rational basis for expectations about how the others will react, and to have some hope for future reciprocity in exchange for current generosity? There are probably no encompassing truths to be discovered on this score, although it is likely that community values and standards are assets that take work to build and care to maintain. If increasing mobility threatens the cohesion and continuity of smaller communities, this poses a double challenge to those who see social and institutional capital as worth maintaining. On the one hand there is potential for spreading the ambit and power of more globally encompassing values and social institutions; on the other hand is the possibility of strengthening local networks to make them more accepting of newcomers and less likely to fall to lowest-common-denominator standards in the face of increasing heterogeneity. An additional risk is that desire to build social cohesion in one community will tempt leaders to use the dangerous cement offered by the ease with which those on the other sides of borders or gates can be assigned the roles of villains or scapegoats. This is a darker side of regarding national borders as lines of demarcation for organizing searches and exchanges.

The second, and quite different, case for efficient market segmentation was made by Richardson, who saw inherent difficulties in establishing an orderly and efficient investment process if opportunities were equally available and equally known to all, while being finite in scope.[23] As he put the case, an opportunity available to one, but equally known to and accessible by all, becomes an opportunity for none. He interpreted the case as setting limits to the desirable extent of competition in circumstances where investment requires long-term irreversible commitments.

National borders have been shown to segment investors and traders into pools of interest and primary activity. This segmentation provides the economic distance argued for by Richardson, serving to give to investors a field of operations in which investment opportunities are more easily and quickly known to them. This gives them some assurance that if they move quickly and with sufficient efficiency the opportunity will remain theirs to exploit. If the system works well, the local providers, with their special knowledge of nearby tastes and opportunities, have the chance to move earlier and more efficiently than more ill-informed investors coming from further afield.

There are limits to the local market power provided by distance and national borders, and this is just as well. The ability of new investors to challenge local fiefdoms is critical to reaping the efficiency gains from a market system. The point of the Richardson argument is that some degree of market segmentation is required to produce an appropriate balance of efficient investment and nonexploitive pricing. Geography and national borders have traditionally acted to provide such segmentation.

Is There a Right Amount of Border Effect?

The material presented in this book has been as factual as I could make it, attempting to measure the size and extent of border effects. These border influences have been found to be surprisingly large, pervasive, and durable. There are also some downward

23. See Richardson (1959, 1960). The point has been made slightly differently, and more recently, by Dixit and Pindyck (1994), who show that industry uncertainty coupled with irreversibility leads a competitive industry to invest less than would a monopolistic industry facing the same uncertainty, for essentially the same reasons spelled out twenty-five years earlier by Richardson. The geographic or national separation of market information is a way of increasing the certainty with which firms can predict the risks that other firms will respond simultaneously to the same investment opportunity.

trends in border effects, especially among those developing countries where the current levels of border effects are highest.

Now it is time to be more speculative, and to ask if the current levels of border effects are too high or too low. If either, by how much, and what should be done to improve the situation? Would the global economy serve the world's people better if it were to become a seamless web in which national borders no longer matter much for the distribution and nature of economic activity? There is a widespread belief that this tight global economy already exists, but the evidence shows that such a perception is dramatically mistaken. This makes it even more important to ask why the border effects are there, and why they remain so large even where there are few if any formal border barriers to support them. Conclusions about the reasons for and implications of the currently large border effects must precede judgments about the many national and international policies that in some way might influence border effects.

Although the evidence about the size and pervasiveness of border effects may be convincing, the basis for judgments about the causes and implications is much more limited. Some further speculation seems worthwhile, if only to help show where future research should be directed.

What sort of framework would help to make sense of the facts? To explain the basic features of the evidence I have summarized in this book, any framework should include some types and levels of border effects that impose net costs on the residents of the enclosed national economies, and perhaps also on their potential trading partners. This is necessary because of the evidence suggesting that sufficiently open countries find themselves able to close the gaps in technology and standards of living between themselves and richer countries. How open is open enough to allow the important information to be accessible? Do diminishing returns to openness set in after some point? Are there competing forces at play, with the right amount of openness depending on a trade-off whose precise nature might differ from time to time and from country to country?

If there is a right amount of openness, determined by offsetting forces, what are the most likely factors to be set against the presumption that access to more knowledge is a good thing? However the explanation is couched, it should depend upon national differences in tastes, institutions, and values, coupled with costs of information, costs of transactions that increase with distance (with borders having a distance equivalence), and the costs of network failure in complex systems.

A typical economy with an "appropriate" amount of border effect would probably have unfettered access to global and international knowledge stocks, and unrestricted rights to travel and trade across national borders. Its equilibrium patterns of travel and trade may continue to show border effects of the sort in evidence among the OECD countries at the end of the twentieth century.[24] If so, it would be because the costs of information are such that local networks are more effective than global ones for meeting and responding to local changes in tastes or circumstances.

Distance is important in separating markets, but the border effects so much studied in this book are measured beyond the costs of distance. Thus if border effects are to be a continuing feature of economic relations there must be something either intrinsic or enduring about national borders as boundaries of groups of people with sufficiently common tastes, values, and shared experiences so as to provide an economic logic for participants in decentralized economic systems to use national borders as important lines of demarcation.

Given that some separation over space may make economic sense for the design and operation of a decentralized economy, the size and pervasiveness of current border effects may be sufficient to make them likely future lines of demarcation. It is well understood in economic geography that cities are located where they are because of events long past, even if, like the never-adopted alternatives to the standard QWERTY typewriter keyboard, there are

24. Alesina, Spolaore, and Wacziarg (1997) extend an analysis of this sort to consider what will happen to equilibrium country size as openness increases. They argue that since country size and openness are alternative ways of getting gains from trade, more openness means that countries will become more numerous and smaller, to permit groups of national citizens to have more in common with each other. The analysis in the text asks a different question: For given countries, what will be the equilibrium degree of international economic interdependence?

other designs or patterns of activity that would make more sense if only it were possible to start again with a clean slate.[25] In order for cities or national boundaries to endure, however, they must not foreclose too many attractive options.

If national boundaries are to endure as important dividing lines in economic space, this implies that economic shocks will spill over national boundaries less easily than they spill over otherwise similar geographic distance. This is more likely to be a preferred outcome if the residents of a country are more willing to share and redistribute among themselves than with those in other countries. This may be likely if they know more about, and share more history and institutions with, their fellow residents of the same country. It was striking, but perhaps not surprising, that the Manitoba floods of 1997 and the Saguenay flood of 1996 drew large flows of voluntary contributions from across Canada, but not from across the border, while the 1997 upstream flooding in North Dakota, before the Red River crests passed over the border into Manitoba, attracted official and private support from the U.S. side of the border. This border effect for benevolence probably depended more on the operation of the media and the infrastructure of public and private aid than on lack of goodwill for those hard hit in another country. But with disaster everywhere, even the best of Samaritans must make choices. In facing this need to be selective, people seem to respond first and most generously to aid those individuals and groups whom they know most about, and for whom they have the strongest combination of responsibility and fellow feeling. Richard Freeman's study of the supply of volunteer labor in the United States shows that the personal, business, and volunteer networks are intertwined, with volunteers contributing their efforts when asked to do so by friends and colleagues.[26]

If the facts about the boundary effects of responses to natural disasters come as no surprise, should it not be equally natural to expect the same borders to influence commercial searches and networks? The economist's traditional response would be "but

25. For discussion of the importance of path dependence on economic geography, see Krugman (1991). For an application of similar reasoning to explain hysteresis in trade patterns, see Grossman and Helpman (1993).

26. See Freeman (1997).

only if there are not too many high-value transborder transactions thereby ignored." Hence the need for some form of diminishing returns to international integration. If increasing product variety, long the staple basis for two-way trade in manufacturing, eventually starts to pall on consumers facing one brand too many, and if local markets are already attaining adequate economies of scale, then the lower densities of transborder transactions may not leave much on the table by way of unrealized gains from trade.

Evaluating the evidence on this score is not easy. One test might be to compare incomes in Canada and the United States. If it were the case that interstate trading linkages were as tight in the United States as interprovincial ones are in Canada, a supposition that lack of data makes untestable, then the large border effect between the two countries means that Canadian firms and individuals typically trade less than Americans. If that lower density of total trade reflected important lost opportunities, then one would expect to find per capita income differences between the two countries to be larger and longer sustained than they have been. Another crude test is to look at the consequences for trade and productivity of the Canada–U.S. FTA of 1988. As already seen, two-way manufacturing trade between Canada and the United States increased dramatically in the early 1990s, but there has not been a corresponding increase in manufacturing productivity.[27]

If this result is confirmed over the longer term, it suggests that diminishing returns to two-way trade in manufacturing may set in when border effects get as low as they were before the FTA between Canada and the United States.[28] If that should turn out to be the case, then border effects may remain at levels not unlike those among the OECD countries at the end of the twentieth century without causing any material loss of welfare. If so, then

27. Head and Ries (1997a, 1997b).
28. Recent research by Baldwin and Caves (1997) suggests that efficiency gains may be reaped from increased international exposure, even for the already open OECD economies. They find, looking across 110 Canadian manufacturing industries, that greater exposure to import competition is associated with higher average efficiency levels. They also find that greater exposure to international competition is associated with increased industry turbulence, as measured by the exit and entry of firms. They interpret the former result as supporting the case for further increases in openness, while noting that the balance of costs and benefits from increased turbulence is more problematic.

mutual reliance on common institutions, values, and infrastructure within nation-states is likely to continue, and to provide some underlying logic for continued separation of economic activities along national borders.

It is too early to rush to judgment about whether national border effects are relics of policy mistakes or evidence of efficient specialization of economic and social networks. For the majority of the world's population living in relatively closed economies, further reductions in border effects are likely to hold more promise than peril. For the industrial countries already tightly bound into the global trading system, there are likely to be fewer gains from further globalization. In either case, it must be expected that international frameworks and codes of conduct are likely to be proposed to increase the gains and decrease the costs of increasing mobility.[29] Evidence and judgments on these questions lie beyond the scope of this book, which will have succeeded if it has managed to convince the reader that border effects are too large to be ignored and too complex to be easily classed as good or bad.

29. Rodrik (1997) offers the example of internationally agreed tax rates on capital as a means of maintaining equitable and efficient relative rates of tax on labor when international mobility of capital increases faster than that of labor. Similar proposals have been made with respect to environmental and labor standards.

References

Abramovitz, Moses. 1979. "Rapid Growth Potential and its Realization: The Experience of Capitalist Economies in the Postwar Period." In *Economic Growth and Resources: Proceedings of the Fifth World Congress of the International Economic Association Held in Tokyo, Japan, 1977,* edited by E. Malinvaud, 1–30. London: Macmillan.

———. 1986. "Catching Up, Forging Ahead, and Falling Behind." *Journal of Economic History* 46(2): 385–406.

———. 1990. "The Catch-up Factor in Postwar Economic Growth." *Economic Inquiry* 28(1): 1–18.

Aitken, Norman D. 1973. "The Effect of EEC and EFTA on European Trade: A Temporal Cross-Section Analysis." *American Economic Review* 63(5): 881–92.

Aizenman, Joshua. 1997. "International Portfolio Diversification with Generalized Expected Utility Preferences." NBER Working Paper 5965. Cambridge, Mass.: National Bureau of Economic Research.

Alchian, Armen, and Harold Demsetz. 1972. "Production, Information Costs, and Economic Organization." *American Economic Review* 62(5): 777–95.

Alesina, Alberto, and Dani Rodrik. 1994. "Distributive Politics and Economic Growth." *Quarterly Journal of Economics* 109(2): 465–90.

Alesina, Alberto, Enrico Spolaore, and Romain Wacziarg. 1997. "Economic Integration and Political Disintegration." NBER Working Paper 6163. Cambridge, Mass.: National Bureau of Economic Research.

Almeida, Paul and Bruce Kogut. 1998. "The Economic Sociology of the Geographic Localization of Ideas and the Mobility of Patent Holders." *American Sociological Review* (forthcoming).

Almond, Gabriel A., and Sidney Verba. 1963. *The Civic Culture: Political Attitudes and Democracy in Five Nations.* Princeton University Press.

Anderson, James E. 1979. "A Theoretical Foundation for the Gravity Equation." *American Economic Review* 69(1): 106–16.

Anderson, Michael A., and Stephen L. Smith. 1996. "Do National Borders Really Matter? A Reconsideration of Canada–U.S. Regional Trade." Paper presented to the Conference of the Southern Economics Association. Washington, D.C. November.

———. 1997. "Canadian Provinces in World Trade: Engagement and Detachment." Lexington, Ky.: Washington and Lee University. January.

Armington, Paul. 1969. "A Theory of Demand for Products Distinguished by Place of Production." *IMF Staff Papers* 16(1): 159–78.

Armstrong, Harvey W., V. N. Balasubramanyam, and Mohammed A. Salisu. 1996. "Domestic Savings, Intra-National and Intra-European Union Capital Flows, 1971–1991." *European Economic Review* 40(6): 1229–35.

Arrow, Kenneth J., and others. 1961. "Capital-Labor Substitution and Economic Efficiency." *Review of Economics and Statistics* 43: 225–50.

Backus, David K., Patrick J. Kehoe, and Timothy J. Kehoe. 1992. "In Search of Scale Effects in Trade and Growth." *Journal of Economic Theory* 58(2): 377–409.

Baldwin, John R., and Richard E. Caves. 1997. "International Competition and Industrial Performance: Allocative Efficiency, Productive Efficiency and Turbulence." Analytical Studies Branch Research Paper Series 108. Ottawa: Statistics Canada.

Bank of Canada. 1969. *Statistical Summary: 1969 Supplement.* Ottawa.

Barro, Robert J. 1991. "Economic Growth in a Cross Section of Countries." *Quarterly Journal of Economics* 106(2): 407–43.

Barro, Robert J., and Jong-Wha Lee. 1993. "International Comparisons of Educational Attainment." *Journal of Monetary Economics* 32(3): 363–94.

Barro, Robert J., and Xavier Sala-i-Martin. 1995. *Economic Growth.* McGraw-Hill.

Baumol, William J. 1986. "Productivity Growth, Convergence and Welfare: What the Long-Run Data Show." *American Economic Review* 76(5): 1072–85.

Baumol, William J., and Edward N. Wolff. 1988. "Productivity Growth, Convergence and Welfare: Reply." *American Economic Review* 78(5): 1155–59.

Baxter, Marianne, and Mario J. Crucini. 1993. "Explaining Saving-Investment Correlations." *American Economic Review* 83(3): 416–36.

Baxter, Marianne, and Urban J. Jermann. 1997. "The International Diversification Puzzle Is Worse Than You Think." *American Economic Review* 87(1): 170–80.

Bayoumi, Tamin, David Coe, and E. Helpman. 1998. "R&D Spillovers and Global Growth." *Journal of International Economics* 42 (forthcoming).

Bayoumi, Tamin, and Barry Eichengreen. 1995. "Is Regionalism Simply a Diversion? Evidence From the Evolution of the EC and EFTA." NBER Working Paper 5283. Cambridge, Mass.: National Bureau of Economic Research.

Bayoumi, Tamin, and Michael W. Klein. 1995. "A Provincial View of Capital Mobility." NBER Working Paper 5115. Cambridge, Mass.: National Bureau of Economic Research.

Bayoumi, Tamin, and Andrew Rose. 1993. "Domestic Saving and Intra-National Capital Flows." *European Economic Review* 37(6): 1197–1202.

Ben-David, Dan. 1993. "Equalizing Exchange: Trade Liberalization and Income Convergence." *Quarterly Journal of Economics* 108(3): 653–79.

————. 1994. "Income Disparity among Countries and the Effect of Freer Trade." In *Economic Growth and the Structure of Long-Term Development: Proceedings of the IEA Conference Held in Varenna, Italy,* edited by Luigi L. Pasinetti and Robert M. Solow, 45–64. Macmillan.

————. 1996. "Trade and Convergence among Countries." *Journal of International Economics* 40(3–4): 279–98.

Ben-David, Dan, and A. Rahman. 1996. "Technological Convergence and International Trade." CEPR Working Paper 1359. London: Centre for Economic Policy Research.

Ben-Porath, Yoram. 1980. "The F-Connection: Families, Friends and Firms and the Organization of Exchange." *Population and Development Review* 6(1): 1–30.

Bergstrand, Jeffrey H. 1985. "The Gravity Equation in International Trade: Some Microeconomic Foundations and Empirical Evidence." *Review of Economics and Statistics* 67(3): 474–81.

————. 1989. "The Generalized Gravity Equation, Monopolistic Competition, and the Factor-Proportions Theory in International Trade." *Review of Economics and Statistics* 71(1): 143–53.

Bernard, Andrew B., and Steven N. Durlauf. 1996. "Interpreting Tests of the Convergence Hypothesis." *Journal of Econometrics* 71(1–2): 161–73.

Bernard, Andrew B., and Charles I. Jones. 1996. "Productivity and Convergence across U.S. States and Industries." In *Long Run Economic Growth,* edited by Steven Durlauf, John F. Helliwell, and Baldev Raj, 113–36. Heidelberg: Physica-Verlag.

Bernstein, Jeffrey I., and Xiaoyi Yan. 1997. "International R&D Spillovers between Canadian and Japanese Industries." *Canadian Journal of Economics* 30(2): 276–94.

Bhagwati, Jagdish N., and Carlos A. Rodriguez. 1975. "Welfare-Theoretical Analyses of the Brain Drain." *Journal of Development Economics* 2(3): 195–221.

Borjas, George. 1994. "The Economics of Immigration." *Journal of Economic Literature* 32: 1667–1717.

————. 1995a. "Ethnicity, Neighborhoods and Human Capital Externalities." *American Economic Review* 85(3): 365–90.

————. 1995b. "The Economic Benefits from Immigration." *Journal of Economic Perspectives* 9(2): 3–22.

Bosworth, Barry. 1995. Review of *Capital Mobility: The Impact on Consumption, Investment and Growth,* edited by Leonardo Leiderman and Assaf Razin (1994, Cambridge University Press). *Journal of Economic Literature* 33(4): 1990–91.

Bottazzi, Laura, Paolo Pesenti, and Eric van Wincoop. 1996. "Wages, Profits and the International Portfolio Puzzle." *European Economic Review* 40(2): 219–54.

Bröcker, Johannes. 1984. "How Do International Trade Barriers Affect Interregional Trade?" In *Regional and Industrial Development Theories, Models and Empirical Evidence,* edited by Åke E. Andersson, Walter Isard, and Tonu Puu, 219–39. Studies in Regional Science and Urban Economics Series, vol. 11. New York: Elsevier Science, 219–39.

————. 1997. "How Would an EU-Membership of the Visegrad Countries Affect Europe's Economic Geography?" Diskussionsbeiträge aus dem Institut für Wirtschaft und Verkehr Nr. 1/97. Dresden: Technische Universität Dresden.

Bruno, Michael. 1993. "Inflation and Growth in an Integrated Approach." NBER Working Paper 4422. Cambridge, Mass.: National Bureau of Economic Research.

Bryant, Ralph C., and others, eds. 1988. *Empirical Macroeconomics for Interdependent Economies.* Brookings.

Bureau of the Census. 1990. *Census of the Population.* U.S. Department of Commerce.

Carrington, William J., Enrica Detragiache, and Tara Vishwanath. 1996. "Migration with Endogenous Moving Costs." *American Economic Review* 86(4): 909–30.

Casella, Alessandra. 1992. "On Markets and Clubs: Economic and Political Integration of Regions with Unequal Productivity." *American Economic Review* 82(2): 115–21.

Cesarano, Filippo. 1997. "Currency Areas and Equilibrium." *Open Economies Review* 8(1): 51–59.

Coakley, Jerry, Farida Kulasi, and Ron Smith. 1996. "Current Account Solvency and the Feldstein-Horioka Puzzle." *Economic Journal* 106 (May): 620–27.

Coe, David T., and Elhanan Helpman. 1995. "International R&D Spillovers." *European Economic Review* 39(5): 859–87.

Coe, David T., Elhanan Helpman, and Alexander W. Hoffmaister. 1997. "North-South R&D Spillovers." *Economic Journal* 107 (January): 134–49.

Coleman, James S. 1990. *Foundations of Social Theory.* Harvard University Press.

Cumby, Robert E., and Maurice Obstfeld. 1984. "International Interest Rate and Price Level Linkages under Flexible Exchange Rates: A Review of Recent Evidence." In *Exchange Rate Theory and Practice,* edited by John F. O. Bilson and Richard G. Marston, 121–51. University of Chicago Press.

Dasgupta, Partha. 1988. "Trust as a Commodity." In *Trust: Making and Breaking Cooperative Relations,* edited by Diego Gambetta, 49–72. New York: Blackwell.

Davis, Donald R., and others. 1997. "Using International and Japanese Regional Data to Determine When the Factor Abundance Theory of Trade Works." *American Economic Review* 87(3): 421–46.

Deardorff, Alan. 1998. "Determinants of Bilateral Trade: Does Gravity Work in a Frictionless World?" In *The Regionalization of the World Economy,* edited by Jeffrey A. Frankel, 7–28. University of Chicago Press.

De Grauwe, Paul. 1988. "Exchange Rate Variability and the Slowdown in Growth of International Trade." *IMF Staff Papers* 35(1): 63–84.

Dekle, Robert. 1996. "Savings-Investment Associations and Capital Mobility: On the Evidence from Japanese Regional Data." *Journal of International Economics* 41(1–2): 53–72.

De Long, J. Bradford. 1988. "Productivity Growth, Convergence and Welfare: Comment." *American Economic Review* 78(5): 1138–54.

Dixit, Avinash K., and Robert S. Pindyck. 1994. *Investment under Uncertainty.* Princeton University Press.

Dollar, David. 1992. "Outward-Oriented Developing Countries Really Do Grow More Rapidly: Evidence from 95 LDCs, 1976–1985." *Economic Development and Cultural Change* 40(3): 523–44.

Dollar, David, and Edward N. Wolff. 1988. "Convergence of Industrial Labor Productivity among Advanced Economies 1963–1982." *Review of Economics and Statistics* 70(4): 549–58.

Dollar, David, Edward N. Wolff, and William J. Baumol. 1987. "The Factor-Price Equalization Model and Industry Labor Productivity: An Empirical Test across Countries." In *Empirical Methods for International Trade,* edited by Robert C. Feenstra, 23–47. MIT Press.

Dooley, Michael, Jeffrey Frankel, and Donald J. Mathieson. 1987. "International Capital Mobility: What Do Saving-Investment Correlations Tell Us?" *International Monetary Fund Staff Papers* 34: 503–30.

Dowrick, Steve, and Norman Gemmell. 1991. "Industrialisation, Catching Up and Economic Growth: A Comparative Study across the World's Capitalist Economies." *Economic Journal* 101 (March): 263–75.

Dowrick, Steve, and Duc-Tho Nguyen. 1989. "OECD Comparative Economic Growth 1950–85: Catch-Up and Convergence." *American Economic Review* 79(5): 1010–30.

Dowrick, Steve, and John Quiggin. 1997. "True Measures of GDP and Convergence." *American Economic Review* 87(1): 41–64.

Durlauf, Steven N., and Paul A. Johnson. 1995. "Multiple Regimes and Cross-Country Growth Behavior." *Journal of Applied Econometrics* 10(4): 365–84.

Eaton, Jonathan, and Samuel Kortum. 1996. "Trade in Ideas: Patenting and Productivity in the OECD." *Journal of International Economics* 40(3–4): 251–78.

Edwards, Sebastian. 1993a. "Trade Policy, Exchange Rates and Growth." NBER Working Paper 4511. Cambridge, Mass.: National Bureau of Economic Research.

———. 1993b. "Openness, Trade Liberalization, and Growth in Developing Countries." *Journal of Economic Literature* 31(3): 1358–93.

———. 1997. "Openness, Productivity and Growth: What Do We Really Know?" NBER Working Paper 5978. Cambridge, Mass.: National Bureau of Economic Research.

Engel, Charles. 1993. "Real Exchange Rates and Relative Prices: An Empirical Investigation." *Journal of Monetary Economics* 32: 35–50.

Engel, Charles M., and Kenneth M. Kletzer. 1989. "Saving and Investment in an Open Economy with Non-Traded Goods." *International Economic Review* 30(4): 735–52.

Engel, Charles, and J. H. Rogers. 1996. "How Wide Is the Border?" *American Economic Review* 86 (December): 1112–25.

———. 1997. "Violating the Law of One Price: Should We Make a Federal Case Out of It?" Paper prepared for the CEPR-PIES Conference on Market Integration and Real Exchange Rates. May.

———. 1998. "Regional Patterns in the Law of One Price: The Roles of Geography vs. Currencies." In *The Regionalization of the World Economy,* edited by Jeffrey A. Frankel, 153–83. University of Chicago Press.

Fagerberg, Jan. 1994. "Technology and International Differences in Growth Rates." *Journal of Economic Literature* 32(3): 1147–75.

Feder, Gershon. 1980. "Alternative Opportunities and Migration: Evidence from Korea." *Annals of Regional Science* 14(1): 1–11.

Feldstein, Martin S. 1994. "Tax Policy and International Capital Flows." Bernhard Harms Lecture, Institut für Weltwirtschaft an der Universität Kiel.

Feldstein, Martin S., and Philippe Bacchetta. 1991. "National Saving and International Investment." In *National Saving and Economic Performance,* edited by D. D. Bernhein and J. B. Shoven, 201–20. University of Chicago Press.

Feldstein, Martin S., and Charles Horioka. 1980. "Domestic Saving and International Capital Flows." *Economic Journal* 90 (June): 314–29.

Finn, Mary G. 1990. "On Savings and Investment Dynamics in a Small Open Economy." *Journal of International Economics* 29(1–2): 1–21.

Fischer, Stanley. 1993. "The Role of Macroeconomic Factors in Growth." *Journal of Monetary Economics* 32(3): 485–512.

Fitzpatrick, Gary L., and Marilyn J. Modlin. 1986. *Direct-Line Distances.* Metuchen, N.J.: Scarecrow Press.

Foot, David K., and William J. Milne. 1984. "Net Migration Estimation in an Extended, Multiregional Gravity Model." *Journal of Regional Science* 24(1): 119–33.

Frankel, Jeffrey A. 1985. "International Capital Mobility and Crowding-Out in the U.S. Economy: Imperfect Integration of Financial or of Goods Markets?" In *How Open Is the U.S. Economy?* edited by R. W. Hafer, 33–67. Lexington Books.

———. 1991. "Quantifying International Capital Mobility in the 1980s." In *National Saving and Economic Performance,* edited by Douglas B. Bernheim and John R. Shoven, 227–60. University of Chicago Press.

———. 1992. "Measuring International Capital Mobility: A Review." *American Economic Review* 82(2): 197–202.

———. 1994. "Introduction." In *The Internationalization of Equity Markets,* edited by Jeffrey A. Frankel, 1–20. University of Chicago Press.

Frankel, Jeffrey A., and Andrew K. Rose. 1996. "A Panel Project on Purchasing Power Parity: Mean Reversion Within and Between Countries." *Journal of International Economics* 40(1–2): 209–24.

Frankel, Jeffrey A., Ernesto Stein, and Shang-Jin Wei. 1995. "Trading Blocs and the Americas: The Natural, the Unnatural and the Supernatural." *Journal of Development Economics* 47(1): 61–95.

Frankel, Jeffrey A., and Shang-Jin Wei. 1993. "Trade Blocs and Currency Blocs." NBER Working Paper 4335. Cambridge, Mass.: National Bureau of Economic Research.

———. 1994. "Yen Bloc or Dollar Bloc? Exchange Rate Policies of the East-Asian Economies." In *Macroeconomic Linkage: Savings, Exchange Rates, and Capital Flows,* edited by Takatoshi Ito and Anne O. Kreuger, 295–329. NBER East Asia Seminar on Economics, vol. 3. University of Chicago Press.

Freeman, Richard B. 1997. "Working for Nothing: The Supply of Volunteer Labor." *Journal of Labor Economics* 15(1): S140–66.

French, Kenneth R., and James M. Poterba. 1991. "Investor Diversification and International Equity Markets." *American Economic Review* 81(2): 222–26.

Froot, Kenneth A., and Kenneth Rogoff. 1995. "Perspectives on PPP and Long-Run Real Exchange Rates." In *Handbook of International Economics,* vol. 3, edited by G. Grossman and K. Rogoff, 1648–88. North-Holland.

Fujiki, Hiroshi, and Yukinobu Kitamura. 1995. "Feldstein-Horioka Paradox Revisited." *Bank of Japan Monetary and Economic Studies* 13(1): 1–16.

Gallup, John L. 1997. "Theories of Migration." Development Discussion Paper 569. Cambridge, Mass.: Harvard Institute for International Development.

Galor, Oded. 1996. "Convergence? Inferences from Theoretical Models." CEPR Discussion Paper 1350. London: Centre for Economic Policy Research.

Gaudry, Marc, U. Blum, and John McCallum. 1996. "A First Gross Measure of Unexploited Single Market Integration Potential." In *Europe's Challenges,* edited by S. Urban, 449–61. Weisbaden: Gabler.

Genovesi, Antonio. 1803. "Lezioni di Economia Civile." In *Scrittori Classici Italiani di Economia Politica,* parte moderna, vol. ix, edited by P. Custodi, 5–228. Milan: Nella stamperia e fonderia di G. G. Destefanis.

Goldberg, Pinelopi K., and Michael M. Knetter. 1997. "Goods Prices and Exchange Rates: What Have We Learned?" *Journal of Economic Literature* 35(3): 1243–72.

Gordon, Roger H., and A. Lans Bovenberg. 1996. "Why Is Capital So Immobile Internationally? Possible Explanations and Implications for Capital Income Taxation." *American Economic Review* 86 (December): 1057–75.

Gould, David M. 1994. "Immigrant Links to the Home Country: Empirical Implications for U.S. Bilateral Trade Flows." *Review of Economics and Statistics* 76(2) (May): 302–16.

Greenwood, Michael J. 1975. "Research on Internal Migration in the United States: A Survey." *Journal of Economic Literature* 13: 397–433.

Greif, Avner. 1992. "Institutions and International Trade: Lessons from the Commercial Revolution." *American Economic Review* 82(2): 128–33.

Grossman, G. M., and E. Helpman. 1993. "Hysteresis in the Trade Pattern." In *Theory, Policy and Dynamics in International Trade: Essays in Honor of Ronald W. Jones,* edited by Wilfred J. Ethier, Elhanan Helpman, and J. Peter Neary, 268–90. Cambridge University Press.

Gylfason, Thorvaldur. 1991. "Inflation, Growth and External Debt: A Review of the Landscape." *World Economy* 14(3): 279–98.

Harrigan, James. 1996. "Openness to Trade in Manufactures in the OECD." *Journal of International Economics* 40(1–2): 23–39.

Harrison, Ann. 1996. "Openness and Growth: A Time-Series, Cross-Country Analysis for Developing Countries." *Journal of Development Economics* 48: 419–47.

Hart, Oliver. 1995. *Firms, Contracts, and Financial Structure.* Oxford: Clarendon Press.

Head, Keith, and John Ries. 1997a. "Market-Access Effects of Trade Liberalization: Evidence from the Canada–U.S. Free Trade Agreement." In *The Effects of U.S. Trade Protection and Promotion Policies,* edited by R. C. Feenstra, 323–42. NBER Project Report Series. University of Chicago Press.

———. 1997b. "Rationalization Effects of Tariff Reductions." Draft working paper.

———. 1998. "Immigration and Trade Creation: Econometric Evidence from Canada." *Canadian Journal of Economics* 31: 47–62.

Helliwell, John F. 1994a. "International Growth Linkages: Evidence from Asia and the OECD." In *Macroeconomic Linkage: Savings, Exchange Rates and Capi-*

tal Flows, edited by T. Ito and A. O. Krueger, 7–28. NBER–East Asia Seminar on Economics, vol. 3. University of Chicago Press.

———. 1994b. "Empirical Linkages between Democracy and Economic Growth." *British Journal of Political Science* 24: 225–48.

———. 1994c. "Trade and Technical Progress." In *Economic Growth and the Structure of Long-Term Development: Proceedings of the IEA Conference Held in Varenna, Italy,* edited by Luigi L. Pasinetti and Robert M. Solow, 253–71. Macmillan.

———. 1995. "Asian Economic Growth." In *Pacific Trade and Investment: Options for the 90s,* edited by W. Dobson and F. Flatters, 17–47. Kingston: John Deutsch Institute, Queen's University.

———. 1996a. "Convergence and Migration among Provinces." *Canadian Journal of Economics* 29 (April): S324–30.

———. 1996b. "Do National Boundaries Matter for Quebec's Trade?" *Canadian Journal of Economics* 29 (August): 507–22.

———. 1996c. "Do Borders Matter for Social Capital? Economic Growth and Civic Culture in U.S. States and Canadian Provinces." NBER Working Paper 5863. Cambridge, Mass.: National Bureau of Economic Research.

———. 1997. "National Borders, Trade and Migration." *Pacific Economic Review* 2(3): 165–85.

Helliwell, John F., and Alan Chung. 1991a. "Macroeconomic Convergence: International Transmission of Growth and Technical Progress." In *International Economic Transactions: Issues in Measurement and Empirical Research,* edited by Peter Hooper and J. David Richardson, 388–436. NBER Studies in Income and Wealth, vol. 55. University of Chicago Press.

———. 1991b. "Are Bigger Countries Better Off?" In *Economic Dimensions of Constitutional Change,* edited by Robin Boadway, Thomas Courchene, and Douglas Purvis, 346–67. Roundtable Series. Kingston: John Deutsch Institute, Queen's University.

Helliwell, John F., and John McCallum. 1995. "National Borders Still Matter for Trade." *Policy Options/Options Politiques* 16 (July/August): 44–48.

Helliwell, John F., and Ross M. McKitrick. 1998. "Comparing Capital Mobility across Provincial and National Borders." NBER Working Paper. Cambridge, Mass.: National Bureau of Economic Research.

Helliwell, John F., and Robert D. Putnam. 1995. "Economic Growth and Social Capital in Italy." *Eastern Economic Journal* 21(3): 295–307.

Helliwell, John F., Peter H. Sturm, and Gerard Salou. 1985. "International Comparison of the Sources of the Productivity Slowdown, 1973–1982." *European Economic Review* 28(1–2): 157–91.

Helpman, Elhanan. 1984. "Increasing Returns, Imperfect Markets, and Trade Theory." In *Handbook of International Economics,* vol. 1, edited by Ronald Jones and Peter Kenen, 325–65. Handbook in Economics Series, no. 3. North-Holland.

Inglehart, Ronald, Neil Nevitte, and Miguel Basanez. 1996. *The North American Trajectory: Cultural, Economic, and Political Ties among the United States, Canada, and Mexico.* Aldine de Gruyter.

Isard, Peter. 1977. "How Far Can We Push the 'Law of One Price?'" *American Economic Review* 67(5): 942–48.

Ito, Takatoshi, Peter Isard, and Steven Symansky. 1997. "Economic Growth and the Real Exchange Rate: An Overview of the Balassa-Samuelson Hypothesis in Asia." NBER Working Paper 5979. Cambridge, Mass.: National Bureau of Economic Research.

Jansen, W. Jos, and Günther G. Schulze. 1996. "Theory-Based Measurement of the Saving-Investment Correlation with an Application to Norway." *Economic Inquiry* 34(1): 116–32.

Johansson, Borje, and Lars Westin. 1994. "Affinities and Frictions of Trade Networks." *Annals of Regional Science* 28(3): 243–61.

Jorion, Philippe. 1994. "International Equity Transactions and U.S. Portfolio Choice: Comment." In *Internationalization of Equity Markets,* edited by Jeffrey A. Frankel, 216–20. NBER Project Report Series. University of Chicago Press.

Knack, Stephen, and Philip Keefer. 1995. "Institutions and Economic Performance: Cross-Country Tests Using Alternative Institutional Measures." *Economics and Politics* 7: 207–27.

———. 1997a. "Does Social Capital Have an Economic Payoff? A Country Investigation." *Quarterly Journal of Economics* 112(4): 1251–88.

———. 1997b. "Does Inequality Harm Growth Only in Democracies? A Replication and Extension." *American Journal of Political Science* 41: 323–32.

Kravis, Irving B., and Robert E. Lipsey. 1988. "National Price Levels and the Prices of Tradables and Nontradables." *American Economic Review* 78(2): 474–78.

Krugman, Paul. 1991. *Geography and Trade.* Gaston Eyskens Lecture Series. MIT Press and Leuven University Press.

Leamer, Edward E. 1988. "Measures of Openness." In *Trade Policy Issues and Empirical Analysis,* edited by Robert E. Baldwin, 147–200. NBER Conference Report Series. University of Chicago Press.

Lee, Jong-Wha. 1993. "International Trade, Distortions, and Long-Run Economic Growth." *IMF Staff Papers* 40(2): 299–328.

Levine, Ross, and David Renelt. 1992. "A Sensitivity Analysis of Cross-Country Growth Regressions." *American Economic Review* 82(4): 942–63.

Levine, Ross, and Sara J. Zervos. 1993. "What Have We Learned about Policy and Growth from Cross-Country Growth Regressions?" *American Economic Review Papers and Proceedings* 83(2): 426–30.

Lewis, K. Karen. 1995. "Puzzles in International Financial Markets." In *Handbook of International Economics,* vol. 4. North-Holland. Previously NBER Working Paper 4951. Cambridge, Mass.: National Bureau of Economic Research, 1994.

Lichtenberg, Frank, and Bruno van Pottelsberghe de la Potterie. 1996. "International R&D Spillovers: A Re-Examination." NBER Working Paper 5668. Cambridge, Mass.: National Bureau of Economic Research.

Linnemann, Hans. 1966. *An Econometric Study of International Trade Flows.* North-Holland.

Lucas, Robert E., Jr. 1988. "On the Mechanics of Economic Development." *Journal of Monetary Economics* 22(1): 3–42.

———. 1990. "Why Doesn't Capital Flow from Rich to Poor Countries?" *American Economic Review* 80(2): 92–96.

McCallum, John. 1995. "National Borders Matter: Canada–U.S. Regional Trade Patterns." *American Economic Review* 85 (June): 615–23.

Mackay, J. Ross. 1958. "The Interactance Hypothesis and Boundaries in Canada: A Preliminary Study." *The Canadian Geographer* 11: 1–8.

Maddison, Angus. 1982. *Phases of Capitalist Development.* Oxford University Press.

Mankiw, N. Gregory, David Romer, and David Weil. 1992. "A Contribution to the Empirics of Economic Growth." *Quarterly Journal of Economics* 107(2): 407–37.

Marston, Richard. 1995. *International Financial Integration: A Study of Interest Differentials Between the Major Industrial Countries.* Cambridge University Press.

Mauro, Paolo. 1995. "Corruption and Growth." *Quarterly Journal of Economics* 110(3): 681–712.

Mintz, Jack M., and Ross S. Preston, eds. 1994. *Infrastructure and Competitiveness.* Roundtable Series. Kingston: John Deutsch Institute, Queen's University.

Murphy, Robert G. 1984. "Capital Mobility and the Relation between Saving and Investment in OECD Countries." *Journal of International Money and Finance* 3(3): 327–42.

Obstfeld, Maurice. 1986. "Capital Mobility in the World Economy: Theory and Measurement." *Carnegie-Rochester Conference Series on Public Policy* 24: 55–104.

———. 1995. "International Capital Mobility in the 1990s." In *Understanding Interdependence: The Macroeconomics of the Open Economy,* edited by Peter B. Kenen, 201–61. Princeton University Press.

Obstfeld, Maurice, and Alan M. Taylor. 1997. "The Great Depression as a Watershed: International Capital Mobility over the Long Run." NBER Working Paper 5960. Cambridge, Mass.: National Bureau of Economic Research.

Ohkawa, Kazushi, and Henry Rosovsky. 1973. *Japanese Economic Growth: Trend Acceleration in the Twentieth Century.* Stanford University Press.

Pagden, Anthony. 1988. "The Destruction of Trust and Its Economic Consequences in the Case of Eighteenth-Century Naples." In *Trust: Making and Breaking Cooperative Relations,* edited by Diego Gambetta, 127–41. New York: Blackwell.

Parsley, David C., and Shang-Jin Wei. 1996. "Convergence to the Law of One Price without Trade Barriers or Currency Fluctuations." *Quarterly Journal of Economics* 111(4): 1211–36.

Persson, Torsten, and Guido Tabellini. 1994. "Is Inequality Harmful for Growth?" *American Economic Review* 84(3): 600–21.

Pesenti, Paolo, and Eric van Wincoop. 1996. "Do Nontraded Goods Explain the Home Bias Puzzle?" NBER Working Paper 5784. Cambridge, Mass.: National Bureau of Economic Research.

Platteau, Jean-Philippe. 1994. "Behind the Market Stage Where Real Societies Exist, Parts I and II." *Journal of Development Studies* 30(3): 533–77, 753–817.

Pöyhönen, Peutti. 1963. "A Tentative Model for the Volume of Trade between Countries." *Weltwirtschaftliches Archiv* 90(1).

Psacharopoulos, George. 1985. "Returns to Education: A Further International Update and Implications." *Journal of Human Resources* 20(4): 583–604.

Pulliainen, Kyosti. 1963. "A World Trade Study: An Econometric Model of the Pattern of the Commodity Flows of International Trade in 1948–60." *Economiska Samfundets, Tidskrift* 16: 78–91.

Putnam, Robert D. 1993. *Making Democracy Work: Civic Traditions in Modern Italy.* Princeton University Press.

———— 1995. "Bowling Alone, Revisited." *The Responsive Community: Rights and Responsibilities* 5(2): 18–33.

————. 1996. "Tuning In, Tuning Out: The Strange Disappearance of Social Capital in America." *PS Political Science and Politics* 28(4): 644–83.

Quah, Danny T. 1996. "Twin Peaks: Growth and Convergence in Models of Distribution Dynamics." *Economic Journal* 106 (July): 1045–55.

Rauch, James E. 1996. "Networks Versus Markets in International Trade." NBER Working Paper 5617. Cambridge, Mass.: National Bureau of Economic Research.

Rice, Tom W., and Jan L. Feldman. 1995. "Civic Culture and Democracy from Europe to America." Mimeo. University of Vermont.

Richardson, George B. 1959. "Equilibrium, Expectations, and Information." *Economic Journal* 69 (June): 223–37.

————. 1960. *Information and Investment: A Study in the Working of the Competitive Economy.* Oxford University Press.

Rodrik, Dani. 1994a. "King Kong Meets Godzilla: The World Bank and the East Asian Miracle." CEPR Discussion Paper 944. London: Centre for Economic Policy Research.

————. 1994b. "Getting Interventions Right: How South Korea and Taiwan Grew Rich." NBER Working Paper 4964. Cambridge, Mass.: National Bureau of Economic Research.

————. 1997. *Has Globalization Gone Too Far?* Institute for International Economics.

Romer, Paul M. 1986. "Increasing Returns and Long-Run Growth." *Journal of Political Economy* 94(5): 1002–37.

————. 1994. "The Origins of Endogenous Growth." *Journal of Economic Perspectives* 8(1): 3–22.

Rostow, Walt Whitman. 1971. *The Stages of Economic Growth: A Non-Communist Manifesto,* 2nd ed. Cambridge University Press.

Sachs, Jeffrey D., and Andrew Warner. 1995. "Economic Reform and the Process of Global Integration." *Brookings Papers on Economic Activity* 1: 1–118.

Sala-i-Martin, Xavier X. 1996a. "The Classical Approach to Convergence Analysis." *Economic Journal* 106 (July): 1019–36.

————. 1996b. "Regional Cohesion: Evidence and Theories of Regional Growth and Convergence." *European Economic Review* 40(6): 1325–52.

Sanso, Marcos, Rogelio Cuairan, and Fernando Sanz. 1993. "Bilateral Trade Flows, the Gravity Equation, and Functional Form." *Review of Economics and Statistics* 75(2): 266–75.

Sapir, Andre. 1981. "Trade Benefits under the EEC Generalized System of Preferences." *European Economic Review* 15(3): 339–55.

Sherwood-Call, Carolyn. 1996. "The 1980s Divergence in State Per Capita Incomes: What Does It Tell Us?" *Federal Reserve Bank of San Francisco Economic Review* 1: 14–25.

Sinn, Stefan. 1992. "Savings-Investment Correlations and Capital Mobility: On the Evidence from Annual Data." *Economic Journal* 102 (September): 1162–70.

Sirowy, Larry, and Alex Inkeles. 1990. "The Effects of Democracy on Economic Growth and Inequality: A Review." *Studies in Comparative International Development* 25: 126–57.

Solow, Robert M. 1956. "A Contribution to the Theory of Economic Growth." *Quarterly Journal of Economics* 70: 65–94.

Summers, Robert, and Alan Heston 1991. "The Penn World Table (Mark 5): An Expanded Set of International Comparisons, 1950–88." *Quarterly Journal of Economics* 106(2): 327–68.

Taylor, Alan M. 1994. "Domestic Saving and International Capital Flows Reconsidered." NBER Working Paper 4892. Cambridge, Mass.: National Bureau of Economic Research.

———. 1995. "Growth and Convergence in the Asia-Pacific Region: On the Role of Openness, Trade and Migration." NBER Working Paper 5276. Cambridge, Mass.: National Bureau of Economic Research.

———. 1996a. "International Capital Mobility in History: Purchasing Power Parity in the Long Run." NBER Working Paper 5742. Cambridge, Mass.: National Bureau of Economic Research.

———. 1996b. "International Capital Mobility in History: The Saving-Investment Relationship." NBER Working Paper 5743. Cambridge, Mass.: National Bureau of Economic Research.

Taylor, Alan M., and Jeffrey G. Williamson. 1994. "Convergence in the Age of Mass Migration." NBER Working Paper 4711. Cambridge, Mass.: National Bureau of Economic Research.

Tesar, Linda L. 1991. "Savings, Investment and International Capital Flows." *Journal of International Economics* 31(1–2): 55–78.

Tesar, Linda L., and Ingrid M. Werner. 1994. "International Equity Transactions and U.S. Portfolio Choice." In *The Internationalization of Equity Markets,* edited by Jeffrey A. Frankel, 185–216. NBER Project Report Series. University of Chicago Press.

———. 1998. "The Internationalization of Securities Markets since the 1987 Crash." *Brookings-Wharton Papers on Financial Services* 1: 283–351.

Thoumi, Francisco E. 1989. "Bilateral Trade Flows and Economic Integration in Latin America and the Caribbean." *World Development* 17(3): 421–29.

Trefler, Daniel. 1995. "The Case of the Missing Trade and Other Mysteries." *American Economic Review* 85(5): 1029–46.

Treyz, George I., and others. 1993. "The Dynamics of U.S. Internal Migration." *Review of Economics and Statistics* 75: 209–14.

Uppal, Ramam. 1992. "The Economic Determinants of the Home Country Bias in Investors' Portfolios: A Survey." *Journal of International Financial Management and Accounting* 3: 171–89.

Wei, Shang-Jin. 1996. "Intra-national Versus International Trade: How Stubborn Are Nations in Global Integration?" NBER Working Paper 5531. Cambridge, Mass.: National Bureau of Economic Research.

Wei, Shang-Jin, and David C. Parsley. 1995. "Purchasing Power *Dis*parity during the Floating Rate Period: Exchange Rate Volatility, Trade Barriers and Other Culprits." NBER Working Paper 5032. Cambridge, Mass.: National Bureau of Economic Research.

Williamson, Oliver E. 1989. "Transaction Cost Economics." In *Handbook of Industrial Organization*, vol. 1, edited by Richard Schmalensee and Robert D. Willig, 135–82. Amsterdam: Elsevier.

Wolf, Holger C. 1997. "Patterns of Intra- and Inter-State Trade." NBER Working Paper 5939. Cambridge, Mass.: National Bureau of Economic Research.

World Bank. 1993. *The East Asian Miracle: Economic Growth and Public Policy.* Oxford University Press.

Yamori, Nobuyoshi. 1995. "The Relationship between Domestic Savings and Investment: The Feldstein-Horioka Test Using Japanese Regional Data." *Economics Letters* 48(3–4): 361–66.

Young, Alwyn. 1992. "A Tale of Two Cities: Factor Accumulation and Technical Change in Hong Kong and Singapore." In *NBER Macroeconomics Annual 1992*, edited by Olivier Jean Blanchard and Stanley Fischer, 13–54. MIT Press.

———. 1995. "The Tyranny of Numbers: Confronting the Statistical Realities of the East Asian Growth Experience." *Quarterly Journal of Economics* 110(3): 641–80.

Index

CARROLL COLLEGE LIBRARY

2 5052 00643563 2

WITHDRAWN
CARROLL UNIVERSITY LIBRARY